CORPORATE
PROTOCOL

CORPORATE PROTOCOL

A BRIEF CASE FOR BUSINESS ETIQUETTE

by

VALERIE GRANT-SOKOLOSKY

CORPORATE PROTOCOL
A Brief Case for Business Etiquette
ISBN 0-89274-417-0
Copyright by Valerie Grant-Sokolosky
13140 Coit Road - Suite 522
Dallas, Texas 75240
(214) 644-0444

Cartoons by Richard Domingus.

Contents

Acknowledgments

No book is published without the help of many people. I would like to thank those who were diligent in making this book a reality.

First, my husband and best friend, Doug. He not only encouraged me, but actually insisted that the time be devoted to this end.

Next, my precious children - Brandon, my encourager; Jason, my supporter; and Stephanie, my cheerleader.

A special thanks to my clients - companies with whom I work, who have assured me these topics are needed and who consistently purchase this book to use internally for executive development.

And so important to any author are my publishing "families" who believed in this idea and made sure it came into being in the U.S. and internationally.

To all of you, I give thanks and appreciation.

Introduction

Have you ever wondered whether you should stand or not when the president of the company enters the room? Have you ever dropped a fork at lunch and wondered if you should pick it up? Have you ever forgotten someone's name just before you need to introduce him?

Knowledge Breeds Confidence

Where does confidence come from? How can you get more if you do not have enough? Confidence comes from knowledge, preparation, and practice. Would you like to have more confidence that you know the best thing to do most of the time?

You are to be commended for picking up this book because you want to learn the best thing to do. Even if you were born with a silver spoon in your mouth, you may have discovered that you do not necessarily have all the answers of what to do and how best to do it. *Class* is not something that you are born with — it is something that you *learn* and *earn*.

Class Is Learned and Earned

This book teaches more than etiquette and manners. It shows how to acquire discernment during those times when there are no right or wrong answers — when you have to flow with the circumstance, when you have to dig deeply within yourself to react in a gracious and caring way. This book teaches the true meaning of *having class and confidence.*

In my years of working with people of all backgrounds, from the most elite to the new employee struggling to make his or her way in the corporate world, I have found that class isn't something that is determined by status, but by a caring attitude of wanting to create a positive influence in the office or home. A simple gesture of a rose sitting on the night-stand for a guest spending the night can show class whether your home is a mansion or a one-bedroom condominium.

A boss who doesn't berate an employee in front of anyone, but rather takes him aside and points out how something could be done better the next time, is showing class — making the employee feel that only the best is expected because he is worthy of the best. That employer is showing class and keeping the self-image of the employee intact.

Class and professional style come from learning a good sense of conduct in daily business activities and treating others with concern. The business person who knows how to handle any situation with ease and confidence has learned the rules of etiquette and manners. He radiates a self-confidence that comes with this knowledge.

Manners Are People Skills

Besides learning how to gain the confidence to feel at ease in any business situation, there's another reason why what you learn in this book will be extremely important to you. According to Dale Carnegie, an expert in the art of human relations, 15 percent of your success in business is due to your technical knowledge while 85 percent of your success is due to your people skills. *Manners are people skills.*

Many executives have brought situations like the following one to my attention. Joan was a capable and hard-working petroleum engineer who had moved up rapidly in the oil company where she worked. However, she eventually stopped moving up. After staying in the same position for a number of years, she finally asked her supervisor about it. Joan was fortunate to have a male supervisor who was willing to be candid with her.

She was a valued worker who produced not only excellent quality work, but in a commendable quantity. However, the next position up the ladder would involve a great deal of interaction with bankers and consultants who had a direct impact on the company's ability to borrow money for investing in oil and gas production.

Unfortunately, Joan had never developed a professional manner in dealing with business associates. She kept a low profile and had not learned to diplomatically negotiate with fellow professionals. In spite of her excellent technical knowledge and work performance, Joan's move up the corporate ladder had stopped because she lacked people skills!

The Golden Rule Makes Business Sense

Practicing good manners makes business life more enjoyable for everyone because of the courtesy shown to each other. In today's stress-filled world with the ups and downs that are inherent to business, it is nice to find pleasantries. Etiquette that is based on the golden rule makes good business sense.

The essence of this book is: **Do unto others as you would like them to do unto you** and **Don't do unto others anything you would not like done unto you.**

Manners reflect back to this basic rule passed down from centuries ago. Manners have always worked to create the best possible inter-personal skills and always will. But another fact is that rules are made to be broken from time to time, especially rules of etiquette. *If you are ever in doubt as to what to do, always do what will make the other person feel at ease, even if it means breaking a rule.*

As Joan discovered, your day-to-day business style is important in your move up the corporate ladder. It is your knowledge of and skill in using etiquette that makes the difference: knowing what to do, knowing how to do it, and using the correct methods.

Learn the Rules

George Washington was so concerned that people learn good manners that at age 16, he wrote a guideline for courteous behavior. When he became President of the United States, he asked John Adams to help him devise some rules of protocol for use in the White House. Many of these rules still apply today.

Rules have changed in recent years due to a change in women's roles in the corporate world and an availability of higher education for all socio-economic groups, but *there are* written rules of play. Those who know the rules become better players.

The social skills are learned and developed, just as any other skills, by studying a set of rules, then applying and practicing them. Just as surely as an artist produces the color green by combining yellow and blue, good social skills are developed by combining the proper ingredients. Everyone can learn these skills.

Bottom Line Profitability

Quality companies who practice the rules of etiquette within the office attract and keep quality employees. There is harmony and efficiency within the company. The employees produce quality goods and services. A total quality of excellence pervading the company attracts and keeps customers. Efficiency and sales increase which bring increased profit.

*Increased efficiency + increased sales =
increased profit.*

User Friendly

My intent in writing this quick, easy, and user-friendly book which you can carry with you, is to give you some basic guidelines to follow in the most common business situations. Keep this book on your desk or read it on the airplane, quickly refer to it as the need arises, and immediately put the guidelines into practice. You will be surprised at how quickly your people skills develop!

Radiate the self-confidence that comes with knowing what to do and how to do it, and enjoy helping others feel at ease in any situation.

In his definition of *tact*, Gordon Lindsay summed up what good manners are all about:

"Tact is thoughtfulness of others; it is sensitivity to the atmosphere of the moment; it is a combination of interest, sincerity, and brotherly love — giving the other fellow a sense of ease in one's presence. In a word, it is Christian love — the practice of the golden rule."

Part I
Communication

Communication

When you are at a large social or business gathering, how do you enter into the conversation without feeling uncomfortable?

A. Look for a group in which there is someone you know.

B. Go to a small group and try to show that you have a good personality by telling jokes.

C. Enter a group and listen attentively, making a point of remembering names.

D. Walk into a group and wait for someone to include you in the conversation before you say anything.

E. Join a group, and as the conversation opens, enter in as you feel comfortable.

Answers to the questions which appear at the beginning of each part will appear at the end of the final chapter of each part. Answers to the question above appear on p. 50.

1
Verbal
Communication

Does this ever happen to you? As chairman of a business meeting, you assign a project that needs to be done in a certain amount of time. You address each person, giving specific directions, telling each exactly what to do in order to finish the project on time. You then tell the group to report the information they are to gather at the next meeting.

You leave the meeting perfectly assured that you have given instructions clearly and succinctly. However, at the next meeting when you begin asking the participants to report the results of their assignments, you find that one person did not clearly understand the instructions and did not do the task in quite the way you had prescribed. Other people did not even understand that you wanted them to finish their assignments by the next meeting. Other people relate other excuses. All this misunderstanding stems from lack of communication on the part of you giving the instructions or the attendees listening to the instructions.

You can hold a master's degree from Harvard University and have all the knowledge in the world, but if you cannot effectively communicate that knowledge, it has very little value.

To effectively communicate in any conversation, you must say what you mean in a way that the other person can *understand* and *perceive* exactly what you intend.

With the amount of international business being done increasing, taking special care to communicate well is important. Sometimes words we use may have a different meaning to someone from another country. Ann showed her English friend, Irma, some cloth napkins Ann had told Irma she wanted to buy. Irma laughed. "In England *napkin* means 'baby diaper.' You don't have a baby. I wondered why you wanted to buy diapers!"

Your Voice

Speaking clearly and with enthusiasm in your voice can make the message more understandable. Work with your voice to avoid the following:

Monotone.

A high-pitched, whiny voice.

Mumbling.

Speaking with a thick accent.

Talking too fast or too slowly.

Nasal sounds.

To test how you sound to other people, tape record your voice. You will be surprised if you have never heard your voice on tape.

Your professional first impression is important and can be swayed positively or negatively by your use of your voice.

Also increasing your vocabulary will enhance what you say. Learn new words daily and listen intently if you hear one that is strange to you. Look it up to find out its meaning.

Enriching your vocabulary with meaningful words will also keep any tendency toward foul language to a minimum. No matter how angry you become, you never have an excuse to use bathroom talk. Doing this will ruin a professional image.

Careless Speech

"Doncha" for *don't you*

"Whajado" for *what did you do*

"Gunna" for *going to*

"Howjado" for *how do you do*

"Zat so" for *is that so*

Rather than running words together, practice separating them. The following are just a few of many words that are often slurred. Practice saying as clearly as possible the words in the list below and any other words you hear yourself or other people mispronounce.

adult: *a-dult'* not *add-ult*

talking: *talk-ing* not *tawk-in*

athlete: *ath-leet* not *ath-a-leet*

get: *geht* not *git*

wash: *wahsh* not *warsh*

toward: *tord* not *too-ward*

I: *I* not *ah*

government: *guv-ern-mehnt* not *guv-er-mehnt*

21

generally: *jehn-er-ah-lee* not *jehn-ri-lee*

for: *fore* not *fo-war*

Overused and Unprofessional Expressions

1. A few years ago, my children came home from school saying "really" as an exclamation. Hearing that word became quite monotonous, but I actually caught myself using it, too. It made me realize how easily we can form habits of phrasing, often using those phrases or words out of context.

2. The following are often used repetitiously:

"To be honest."

"As a matter of fact."

"Truthfully speaking."

"You know what I mean?"

"Uh-huh" (for yes).

"Uh-uh" (for no).

"Yeah."

3. It is inappropriate for either a man or a woman to refer to a business woman as "girl" or to address her as "honey."

4. Certain locales may use regionalisms, such as "y'all" in Texas. But in the professional world, it is best not to use localisms.

Business Conversation

One of the best methods you can use to communicate well is to see yourself as having to sell your point of view or what you plan to say. You must do everything in your power to make sure that you, as the sender, give a message that is received in the way you intend. To insure that you do this, take the following steps:

1. Learn to say what you mean and mean what you say. I listened to a speaker once who talked on and on for two hours. When I left, I was still not sure what he had come to say! He seemed to go around and around, but never quite hit the point.

When you are talking, think through clearly what you want to say, and say it with only the number of words needed to get the message across. Business people appreciate succinct communication, whether it is written or oral. Remember the rule of KISS — Keep It Short and Sweet.

2. Don't have "I" trouble. Have you ever asked a person how he was, expecting him to answer briefly, then had to listen for minutes because he actually told you? Everyone likes to talk about himself or his family, but too much becomes rude.

Once I called on a client who kept me waiting thirty minutes. When we finally began our conversation, he reminded me of how busy he was. After that, he talked about himself for an hour and a half without stopping. He told me about his accomplishments, his good deeds, and so forth. Doing that was rude, selfish, and showed a lack of concern for anyone but himself. He had "I" trouble.

3. If you are making a speech of any kind in front of a group, be sure to organize your thoughts and, at the beginning, mention the points you plan to cover. Summarize those points at the end by saying something like, "Remember, we covered five reasons today...."

4. In any type of planned business conversation — such as in selling your product, communicating goals to your boss, or interviewing for a job — organize and rehearse your thoughts beforehand. Anticipate questions and have your answers prepared mentally.

Entering a Group Conversation

Many executives who feel right at home in the office feel uncomfortable in a social gathering. Here are some tips to help you feel at ease:

1. Talk about topics other than business.

Include topics the opposite sex can appreciate. One man for whom my husband worked used to graciously talk to me about *my* business, about parts of the country where my husband and I had lived or through which we had traveled, or about general topics such as world events. I appreciated his consideration to include me in the conversation and not just talk business to my husband.

2. Avoid these subjects:

• Your health.

• The cost of things.

• Gossip.

• Off-color jokes.

• Controversial issues when you do not know where the other people in the group stand.

A friend of mine once sat at dinner with someone who held opposite political viewpoints. Not knowing this, my friend expressed a political opinion. The other person reacted negatively and the two became involved in a heated discussion. Dinner was ruined!

Become good at making small talk. Listen and act interested, and you will think of things to say. Asking questions helps. People are flattered when you ask for their opinions.

3. A good conversationalist is cheerful and has a good sense of humor. He reads to stay informed, listens, asks open-ended questions, and is other-centered — he does not have "I" trouble! How to carry on an interesting conversation can be learned!

2
Non-Verbal Communication

The Handshake

The handshake is important — it has become the usual greeting both for a man and a woman. In business or social situations, the woman should feel perfectly at ease in extending her hand to a man or a woman when being introduced.

Give a firm, quick grasp and shake. This shows self-confidence and assurance. Do not ever extend your hand with a few fingers pointed down as if you expect someone to kiss your hand. Shake hands from the elbow, not from the shoulder as if pumping for water. Grasp the other person's hand completely so that the thumbs are interlocked and the hands are completely within each other.

If a woman shakes hands with a man who covers her hand affectionately with his other hand, she can simply take one step backward to politely pull away without making an issue of feeling he was too aggressive.

Body Language

If you are a parent, you know that you do not have to say anything to your child for him to be able to read in your facial expression or through your body posture that you are upset. The way we carry ourselves and gesture with our arms and hands, the facial expressions we use — all give a message without our ever having to open our mouths.

You may think that someone is calm and in control until you notice that he is nervously tapping his fingers on his desk or swinging his foot. Mannerisms can reveal as much about a person as what he says.

The basic body language messages listed below can help you in understanding another person's personality or emotional style.

The Action or Characteristic	The Message
1. Stands tall and erect.	Extrovert. Healthy self-image.
2. Stands slumped with head bowed.	Introvert. Does not feel comfortable in the situation.
3. Uses wide, large gestures.	The person is open and forward with his remarks. Sure of himself.
4. Uses small, close gestures.	Shy or unsure.
5. Remains aloof and distant.	The person tends to stay by himself. May be shy rather than aloof. He could be tense.
6. Leans into an approachable position, a little forward.	The person is outgoing and wants to be included in the conversation.
7. Leans backward and holds head high.	A proud person.
8. Has lots of smile lines.	The person has usually had a happy life. Enjoys people.

26

Much has been written on how to position yourself to show authority and on how to carry yourself to project a positive image. One short man I know seems much taller than he is simply because he walks with his head held high and with an air of self-confidence. When he talks, he maintains good eye contact as well.

Notice your posture, check your walk, make sure you are using gestures that add to, rather than detract from, what you are saying.

One easy rule to keep in mind about hand gestures is to keep them below the neck. This will help you to remember not to twirl your hair, put your hand over your mouth, or play with your moustache — all of which are nervous habits and distracting. Following the suggestions in this chapter will help you seem confident, even when you may be nervous inside.

To enhance good communication, make a point of picking up signals given through body language and adapt your behavior. How someone approaches you may indicate he is under stress or in a hurry. Respond to this message by being crisp and clear. Do not involve the person in idle conversation.

If the person greets you by smiling and extending his hand, you can understand this to mean that the person is relaxed and has time to spend with you. If the person remains seated (which he should not do), or stands and shakes hands from behind his desk, you might interpret this to mean that the person has much on his mind. Respond to what you *see* as well as what you hear.

Personal Space

We all have around us our immediate personal space and resent it being invaded. When you go to the beach, you spread out your towel and maybe set up an umbrella to block out some sun. Isn't it irritating when someone runs over your blanket and invades your "space"? Also, if you have ever been in an exercise class when someone has moved too closely to you in the middle of doing a routine, you may have felt uncomfortable.

If you are in an elevator alone, you will probably stand in the center. If others are in the elevator, you may move to a corner. When several people are in an elevator, they seem to become non-people and stare blankly at the front door or side panel. It is as if people try to occupy and claim some personal space to feel comfortable. They do not want to feel squeezed.

Territory and personal space are usually defined in business settings. When talking to someone, you probably feel most comfortable when you are standing at least an arm's length away. Unless you know the person well, getting too close is offensive.

Respecting personal space is critical when calling on a client. Never invade the other person's territory by putting your personal belongings, such as a briefcase or purse, on his desk. Never pick up something from his desk unless you ask first or unless he offers it to you. The possessions on his desk are to be considered personal. However, you can involve your client when making a presentation and give him a feeling of ownership by asking him to hold a proposal or product as you discuss it with him.

How someone uses his personal space is an interesting topic not often considered as a tool to use in understanding or communicating authority or high status. Through noticing the amount of space a person takes and the way he uses it, you can pick up clues to help you in knowing how to act and communicate with the person. You may encounter several of the following indications of power positions:

1. An oversized desk with chairs directly in front of it signifies a powerful executive who intends to look way across

his or her large desk directly at you. This executive intends to stay in control. Be careful not to overstep his position. Stick to business and respect his space.

2. A corner office with full view of both sides of the outside of the building is usually occupied by the boss. When talking to him, realize that you are with the decision maker and act accordingly.

3. A conference room with a rectangular table and large leather chair at the end is occupied by the person in charge of the meeting.

4. A large office with trophies or certificates on the wall reveals an executive proud of his achievements. You can feel comfortable in commenting on them or asking questions about them since they have been placed to be noticed.

5. An executive who leans back in the chair with legs stretched out in front and hands behind the head is assuming a leadership position — he is commanding more personal space than others and showing an extreme comfort level. This position could also simply be a means of relaxing, so be sure you make assessments based on other non-verbal clues and not on any one signal. All of us might sit in this position at times. But it would not be an appropriate position for a young executive to assume in a business meeting in front of a senior executive.

3
Listening

We can listen at two to three times the speed that most people talk. Because of this, we can think through what is being said — sort it out and edit it — into the most important points to remember. When we train our minds to do this, we are *actively listening*.

One of the best ways to impress your boss with your intelligence is to *listen attentively* when he speaks. Concentrate. Keep good eye contact. A good listener is not only popular everywhere, but after a while, he has learned a lot! My grandmother always said, "Keep quiet — you can't learn anything when you are doing all the talking!"

In a sales situation, the more listening you do, the more likely you will be to make the sale.

John made a sales call on his client, Ben. For an hour and a half, Ben did 80 percent of the talking. John hardly had a chance to present his product and was becoming distressed because the sales call was taking so long. Yet at the end of the time, Ben simply said, "Yes, John, I *do* think we need your product."

Ben had actually talked himself into needing the product without John having to say much. All he did was listen and participate when he could.

One top executive had the habit of always asking opinions of many other people in his company before he came to a final decision. He was not indecisive — he had learned to value the opinions of other people in all areas of the company and knew that he could *learn* from each of them. Listening became an important part of his decision making.

Because we are able to process information much faster than the 200 to 250 words per minute that most people speak, our attention tends to wander. Some statistics show that we spend about 45 percent of our time listening, 30 percent talking, 16 percent reading, and 9 percent writing. If that is true, we are spending almost half our time listening. It is important to know or to sharpen the skills involved in listening, especially if our minds tend to wander. By listening actively we will become much more knowledgeable and better conversationalists.

Caring enough to listen to what others say is a compliment to them. Following the guidelines below will help you in developing the art of listening:

1. Give your full attention.

A Chinese proverb says:

"Tell me, I'll forget,

"Show me, I may remember.

"But involve me, and I'll understand."

Involve yourself in what the other person is saying by giving him your full attention.

• Tune out the noises and distractions around you.

• Look at the person when he speaks. This says you *are* giving him your full attention. When you let your gaze wander away from the individual or around the room, you are obviously either preoccupied or are not interested in the conversation. In either case, the person will notice and might be offended since you are not giving him your full attention.

Not looking someone in the eye can be a habit. A woman I know well talks to me while looking at my right ear, or so it seems to me! When she does that, a strange feeling is created in me which makes talking with her awkward.

In other instances, not looking at someone in the eye might be due to cultural differences or a physical handicap.

2. Comprehend.

• Visualize what is being said. Pictures of meanings can long be remembered over just hearing words.

• Take notes. When in a business meeting or sitting down one-on-one, it is flattering for you to take notes on the points your boss or client is making. This shows you feel the conversation is important and that you want to remember everything being said. Also, it is extremely important to have written notes to refer to later, especially in negotiating.

Listening in a meeting is not always easy. Sometimes conventions and seminars are boring! Remember this: a good speaker will tell you at the beginning of the talk what the topic is and at the end summarize what has been said.

Listen to the highlights or main points of what is said as the day progresses. When the end comes, make sure you have notes on what was summarized. Then you will know you have recorded and will be able to refer to the most important parts of the speech.

• Do not be afraid to ask questions throughout the conversation (or during small meetings) when necessary to understand. However, make sure that you have been actively listening so that you are not asking questions about points which have already been covered.

A seminar on video tape was being given to a small group of people. During the presentation, one member of the class made a comment to his neighbor. Because he had been talking, he missed the point being taught.

A few minutes later, he asked the group leader a question, distracting the entire class. The information he was asking about had been presented while he had been talking. Every few minutes he asked another question, distracting the entire class again. The information he was asking about had been covered in the presentation while he was talking.

By the end of the session, most of the class had missed 80 percent of the material because one person who had not been actively listening asked inappropriate questions.

Also remember that if you are not paying attention to the speaker by talking to your neighbor about a matter that could be discussed later, you are causing your neighbor as well as yourself to miss valuable information. If you just keep in mind to do the most gracious thing, then others in the group will be able to listen attentively as well.

If a point comes up which is unclear, do make statements or ask questions to verify the exact meaning or to understand the conclusions being drawn. If *you* do not understand a point being discussed, there may be other people who are also misunderstanding. A question asked at the appropriate time could clarify a matter and ward off a number of mistakes which could have been made based on wrong conclusions.

During a small group discussion I attended, there were several points I did not understand. At first I felt awkward asking, but decided I needed to know answers in order for the discussion to be meaningful to me. After I had asked the questions, several participants came up to me during the break and said, "I'm so glad you raised those questions. I wondered about them, too."

3. Evaluate.

Assess what you are hearing by looking for the positive in what is being said.

• Try to understand the basics of what the other person is saying.

• Sift out the most important points and begin to formulate your response. This will keep you in control of your end of the discussion.

• As you listen, ask yourself: What should I do with this information? When should I do it? What are my opinions about what I am hearing? What will I gain from learning this information?

4. React.

• Be ready to respond verbally. If someone asks you a question or an opinion, pause a few seconds to think about your response. Be sure to say what you mean. You may regret later bolting into a quick response or giving an answer just for the sake of giving one. Remember that you may be judged by your answer.

React non-verbally to what is being said. If you just keep good eye contact without showing any reaction, the person talking will wonder if you are simply staring without truly understanding. One day I was speaking with a woman who *did* look me in the eye. I was discussing the upcoming business idea I had for a client, but when I quit talking a moment, she responded, "Yes, it *is* supposed to be hotter tomorrow." She was looking, but not listening! The key is to watch for blinking of the eyes. If someone is staring and not blinking, you can bet his thoughts are miles away.

Give a smile, a nod of approval, or make a gesture — whatever comes naturally — but *do* give some kind of response to indicate interest in what is being said.

Some responses that can come in handy are:

"I can see that is important."

"We'll have to give that some further thought."

"I agree with you."

"Isn't that interesting?"

Do not interrupt — this is not a polite way to show that you are actively listening!

Have you ever been in a conversation with a person who keeps interrupting with *his* ideas or thoughts? Soon you feel that the other person is controlling the conversation with his interruptions.

I know a person who has a habit of finishing other people's sentences. She just does not realize she is doing it.

Sometimes I make a game of it with that person. I begin talking then stop. And she keeps going! I make another statement, pause, and she finishes my thought!

Thinking faster than you can talk, the person finishing your sentences already knows what you are going to say before you have had time to say it. This habit of supplying words to a speaker is just as rude as interrupting, particularly for the person who speaks slowly.

Listening on the Telephone

The same rules apply to listening on the phone as for any other kind of listening. But the conversation can be difficult if the person on the other end of the line is speaking without emotion or enthusiasm.

If you are having a hard time listening, make the conversation as brief as possible and ask to meet in person. The communication can be much more active that way.

Quotes about Listening

"Don't talk unless you can improve the silence." (A Vermont Proverb)

"It's all right to hold a conversation, but you should let go of it now and then." (Richard Armour)

"If you don't say anything, you won't be called on to repeat it." (Calvin Coolidge)

Remember: If you were doing the talking, *you* would appreciate someone actively listening and acting as if he were interested in what you had to say. *Do unto others as you would like them to do unto you.*

4
Telephone Techniques

Several years ago, *Fortune* magazine surveyed the heads of top companies to rank the ten worst time wasters. The telephone was number one. The telephone can serve either as the company's most valuable tool or can cause the company to lose customers and money.

According to Nancy Friedman, The Telephone Doctor, more business is lost because of poor service and poor treatment than because of poor product. She notes that an article in *The Wall Street Journal* reported that only 30 percent of the business calls made are completed.

You can see how important it is to a company's business to use good manners and to project professionalism over the telephone. Some basic tools to use in communicating effectively over the telephone follow.

Making A Call

Your first encounter with a client is often by telephone, and your telephone techniques give a positive or negative first impression. Because your listener perceives without the help of non-verbal communication, you must be skilled in expressing yourself verbally through your choice of words, tone of voice, and vocal expression. Practice speaking clearly and with enthusiasm.

1. Write down an outline of the key points you want to discuss.

2. When you call, save the receptionist time by giving her all the information at the beginning: "Hello, this is Mary Smith with Carbondale Realty. May I speak to Arthur Jones?"

3. If the person you are calling is unavailable, leave a message telling the nature of your business. "Would you ask Mr. Jones to call me at 555-3129? I would like to discuss a product he might be interested in seeing."

The receptionist or secretary is instructed to ask the nature of your call. If appropriate, tell her. Feel assured that an executive's secretary is capable of relaying your basic information to her boss; however, reserve the right to discuss the details of the call with him when he returns your call.

Because she is your link in communicating with her boss, a secretary can be your best friend. Of course, be courteous to her at all times.

4. Once you reach the person with whom you want to make an appointment:

• Identify yourself and your company. Ask the person if he has time to talk.

• Move quickly to the point. The client will appreciate your clear and direct approach.

• Have your sales presentation so well defined that you give the client just the right amount of information — say just enough to arrange for an appointment, but not so much as to lose it.

• *Ask* for the appointment. Give your client a choice of times.

• Close pleasantly by saying something such as, "Thank you for your time. I'll look forward to discussing our services with you on Monday."

Answering the Phone

Remember that the way your secretary answers the phone is extremely important. She is the spirit and representative of the company. In the mind of the caller, your secretary *is* the company.

A secretary should:

1. Give a friendly greeting of some kind. "Good morning . . . ."

2. Give the name of the company. "This is XYZ Corporation . . . ."

3. Give her name. "This is Mary Smith speaking . . . ."

4. In answering, the secretary should not overscreen calls. Instead of asking, "Who is calling and to what does this pertain?" the secretary should offer help by saying, "How can I help you?" She should not answer, "May I help you?" because the caller *will* need some kind of help.

5. In her greeting, communicate the mood of your company. If it is a motivational company, the secretary could say, "Good morning! Success Unlimited — have a *great* day!" If it is a law firm, the secretary could be instructed to say, "Hello, John Roberts Law Firm."

6. Always take a message. Never trust that the person will call back.

Transferring a Call

Explain to the person calling *why* you must have him speak to someone else: "You'll need to talk with the receiving department. I'll transfer you if you're able to hold just a moment." Then tell the receiving department about the call. "Nancy, I have Mr. Johnson on the line. He needs to talk to you about his shipment."

When Nancy answers, she should say, "Hello, Mr. Johnson, this is Nancy. How can I help you?" When Nancy answers by calling Mr. Johnson by name, he feels important that she knows *who* is calling.

Putting a Caller on Hold

It is frustrating to be put on hold, and then held and held and held. Before ever putting someone on hold, tell him why you must do so. "I'm sorry, Mr. Johnson, I need to have you hold while I try reaching Ms. Smith." Then *ask his permission* to put him on hold. "Are you *able* to hold just a moment?" If he cannot wait, say, "Please give me your phone number, and I will see to it that Ms. Smith gets this message."

If you have several telephone lines to answer and another call comes in that is important, tell the caller you need to put him on hold, then get back to him *quickly*.

If you are in the middle of a telephone conversation and are interrupted, it is all right to put your client on hold if done politely. When putting someone on hold, just remember to practice the golden rule.

Handling Complaints

1. Let the caller talk without interrupting.

• Listen with undivided attention.

• Be sympathetic.

• Transfer the call to the department or person most easily able to give the solution to the problem.

2. Know your company policies so that *you* can be of some help at the beginning.

3. Never be rude. Instead, realize that the caller is not attacking you personally, but needs to feel that you care about his problem.

4. Take notes of what he is saying so that you clearly understand the reasons for his complaint and can repeat them.

5. Never tell the customer what you *cannot* do, only tell him what you *can* do. Say something like, "I can understand why you are calling, Mr. Johnson. The person who can handle this is not in at the moment. May I take your number? I will see to it that he calls you back today with some information." Or, "I'm sure you will be receiving the shipment soon. But may I transfer you to Mr. Beal in our receiving department? I feel sure he can help you with this."

Executive Calls

1. Always answer the phone calls you receive on a daily basis. If you cannot, ask your secretary to return the call. There is no excuse for simply not answering a phone call. By not answering a call, you are saying, "You are not important enough for me to pay any attention."

2. Never call an executive before 9:00 A.M. or late in the afternoon.

Small Talk

When you are talking with someone who is longwinded, it is perfectly all right to say, "Excuse me, Mary. I have an appointment in a few minutes. Could we continue this conversation later?" Time is important and needs to be respected.

Business Calls at Night

Unless the party requests that you call him at his home, do not. Home time is personal time — not for business.

Efficiency Is Important

You do not often realize the importance of telephone efficiency until the need for communication is crucial. I found this out recently when my mother-in-law died. The only form of communication we had was by telephone.

Just after my mother-in-law was taken to the hospital, I tried to call and check on her condition, but the people in the emergency room could only tell me that she had been moved to her room. The runaround I received from the various nurses' stations and departments was not only frustrating, but totally inefficient.

Within companies, it is of major significance that the people who handle the telephone be continuously fed with information they need to know about any department and its staff. The person then answering the telephone can give the caller specific information such as, "Ms. Evans is at lunch and will be back at 2:00. May I take a message?"

Once I was asked to call a real estate agent to schedule some of my programs for her company. I tried for three days to reach the woman whose name I had been given. Twice I was told by the woman answering the phone that no one by that name worked there. (I did find out later that she was a new agent.)

After checking back with my source, I was assured that the woman I was trying to reach *did* work there. The third time I called, *I had to tell the operator* that I had checked and knew the woman was an employee there. And, sure enough, I was connected. A great deal of business can be lost through that type of inefficiency.

Telephone Tips

1. When calling a business associate or client, identifying yourself first is not only the considerate thing to do, but also lets the other person know that you are a person of worth and value.

2. If a caller does not identify himself, ask, "To whom am I speaking?" If the call is for someone else, ask, "Whom shall I say is calling?" Never say, "Who is this?"

3. If you reach a wrong number, simply say, "I'm sorry." Do not just hang up.

4. Make sure the other person has time to discuss the business you are calling about. If not, ask him for a more convenient time to call back.

5. Realize that very few of us are born with wonderful, resonant, golden voices. Record a conversation and listen to how you sound. You may need to lower the pitch of your voice, speak more slowly, or talk more clearly. Analyze your voice and improve it by practice.

6. As you talk with someone over the phone, always keep a note pad in front of you in order to document the conversation. When you need to remember exactly what you discussed, you can easily refer to the details of the earlier conversation.

5
Written
Communication

Memos to Yourself

I often find myself getting a fantastic idea in the middle of the night or in the car when I am on my way to an appointment. When we are relaxed, the brain tends to "dump out" thoughts and ideas, almost begging to have them written down and out of the way. Our minds do not function well with overload. When we write these things down or record them on tape, the mind says, "Good, I can move on to other information."

I strongly suggest you keep a small battery-operated tape recorder with you in the car, and always carry a pad and pencil at work to note these ideas and lists. Sometimes we think we will remember these thoughts, but when the time comes to recall the information, we have forgotten it. Do not rely on your memory.

Business Letters

A continuing relationship with a client or associate often becomes both a business *and* personal relationship. It is perfectly appropriate to add any personal information within the context of a business letter. Sometimes you may want to handwrite a note at the end.

The most important thing to remember is that you *write* personal letters to business associates to thank them about something. Too often this gracious act is forgotten in the hurrying of day-to-day activities. Your taking time to write a note will be remembered the next time a promotion comes along or a product you have is needed. Do take time to be thoughtful.

Stationery

People often ask me what kind of stationery to use for writing business letters that need a personal touch. Remember that your stationery is a direct reflection of *you* — just as is your dress or suit. Select a stationery that reflects you and your company image.

Traditionally, the basic white, gray, or ivory papers with blue or black ink were popular in the business world. Now companies and entrepreneurs are choosing different colors of paper and ink and expanding the "wardrobe" of stationery.

The more traditional businesses would probably use soft-colored stock paper with a simple design. A law firm would not want bold colors or an unusual typeface. But a company in interior design or fashion might prefer something more outlandish, although still appropriate for business, or an odd-sized paper with a bold typeface on a stronger colored paper stock — a more creative, rather than traditional, approach. (Be sure that the stationery you select fits postal regulations.)

A typical "wardrobe" of stationery might include:

1. Printed stationery with company logo, 8½ x 11 inches (for business writing).

2. Business cards to match the letterhead. (On your business card, state your title. Following your name with several initials that most people would not recognize has no significance and is only confusing.)

3. Printed memo pads (with the company and/or personal name).

4. Monogrammed informal fold-over or singular cards with matching envelopes (to be used for thank you notes, acknowledgments, or personal notes; these do *not* need the business name — only the personal name or initials).

When selecting stationery, choose paper of good quality and a graphic design that reflects what your company offers. Consider different typefaces and colors of paper stock.

Writing the Letter

Be brief. Avoid wordiness. Write in today's modern language, not in formal language as was done many years ago. Replace "Until then, I remain yours truly" with the more informal "Sincerely."

Write a thank you note within the appropriate time frame. Send a note thanking someone for taking you to lunch to discuss business the very day you have had that lunch. A week later is meaningless.

Salutations

Use a person's first name only if you have a close relationship with him or have known him a long time; otherwise, a greeting such as "Dear Mr. Jones" is always appropriate for a young executive who is addressing a senior man. "Dear Bob Jones" is appropriate if you do not want to seem too formal, but do not feel comfortable using only his first name.

If you are writing a woman, always try to find out if she is addressed as "Miss," "Mrs.," or "Ms." If you are not sure, "Ms." is considered appropriate.

Signatures

Simply ending with "Sincerely," as discussed above, is best. However, if writing an official or clergyman, sign "Respectfully yours."

RSVP

RSVP stands for "répondez s'il vous plaît," which is French for "please reply." When you see these initials, respond by phone or mail within one week to indicate whether or not you accept the invitation.

Answers to the question at the beginning of the section: A, C, E.

Part II
Courtesies

Courtesies

When someone enters a group of seated people:

A. The men should stand no matter who enters.

B. Men and women should stand if the person entering is much older or of senior ranking.

C. Only men should stand if the person entering is a clergyman or high official.

D. Men and women should stand if a woman of about the same age as the rest of the group enters.

Answer appears on p. 60.

6
Common Courtesy

To get along well with management as well as with peers, show common courtesy — use good manners and learn people skills. Having good manners in business shows good character, good upbringing, good savvy, and good sense. Elmer G. Leterman says, "Personality can open doors, but only character can keep them open."[1]

I firmly believe one will climb farther up the corporate ladder and *stay* there when he or she practices the golden rule: doing unto others as you would like them to do unto you.

Here are some courtesies to keep in mind daily.

Keep Your Word

If you tell a colleague or client that you are going to do something, such as have a report done on a certain date, follow through. Many people have wonderful start-up skills, then let the ball drop during the project. *Following through* is as important as making the commitment.

---

[1] *On the Upbeat*, 13 Feb., 1986, p. 22.

Answer Calls Daily

There is no excuse for not answering your calls. If you are out of town or too busy, at least have your secretary call to let the party know. Assume if someone calls you, he has a good reason to reach you. Much business is lost because calls are not returned and the person moves on to a competitor. The same is true of answering letters — answer them as soon as possible.

Communicate Openly

• Communicate both with your staff internally and with clients. People are not mind readers. If business is to be accomplished with the least amount of time and the most efficiency, it is good to have constant and open communication.

• Give compliments. One of the most motivating things you can do is to praise an employee when he has done a good job. Everyone responds when he feels appreciated.

Compliment, verbally or by note, the people in your office or your clients (especially competitors) when they receive a promotion or some other honor.

• Acknowledge thoughtfulness. Someone who sends you a gift or note of congratulations will always appreciate a phone call or note of thanks.

Be Sensitive

Be sensitive to personal problems of a colleague or employee. Compassion is not a weakness, but a worthy strength and one that will always be remembered.

• Do not point out individual mistakes in a group. Point out the error in a general way by announcing a guideline or policy. This takes the offense off the individual, but still puts across the point that the particular type of error should not be repeated.

• When invited to an activity, do not bring anyone who is not invited.

Once when I had an open house, I invited a young man whom I was helping up the corporate ladder. He brought an uninvited friend. And to make matters worse, the friend proceeded to give his business card to everyone in the room!

When you are the guest of someone, you should not use the situation selfishly to your own advantage.

Never Burn Bridges

No matter what happened on the job, it is not worth holding grudges and being obvious about it. Forgive and go on.

Once a rude situation developed between a man and me. I remained calm and never let him know how he had hurt my feelings.

Years later when he needed my kind of services, he called me to take part in a big job opportunity. If I had reacted emotionally and become angry, he would not have thought of me professionally later.

Be On Time

Someone once said to me that if you are late, the reason is that you really did not care about going. If you see that you are running late, simply call the party to tell him you will be there at a certain time, and ask if he can wait. If you will be quite late, give him the option of rescheduling and perhaps take him to lunch to make up for the delay.

Be Considerate
When Carrying on
Business During Meals

• Start the meeting with casual conversation. If you have handled the invitation properly by informing your guests of the purpose of the meeting, it will be easy to shift the conversation to business matters.

• If you need to discuss business in a less obvious way, turn the conversation gradually.

• You are trying to build a long-term relationship. If you cannot easily move from one point to another, do not push.

Watch Out For Politics

No one likes someone who is always buttering up the boss. It is obvious he is trying to climb the ladder by always talking to the boss and ignoring his peers.

Do Not Brag

Your accomplishments and talents *are* noticed by your peers without your having to point them out. Constantly talking about yourself bores people.

Be Courteous With Visitors

• Do not keep a guest waiting. If you have made an appointment with someone, be sure to meet with him at that time. Even if the person arranged the meeting to sell you something, remember that his time is valuable, too. If there will be a delay, tell your secretary to let the person waiting know.

• Greet visitors. When someone enters and leaves your office, rise and greet him with a smile and handshake. Offer him a seat. When he is leaving, escort him to the door. These are common courtesies which you would extend in your home and should also be extended in the business atmosphere.

Do Not Overstay

When you are conducting business in another person's office, do so, then leave. Business hours are not the time for small talk or discussing your personal lives. Keep those conversations to the social times at lunch or after work. Being chatty when others are trying to work is annoying.

Follow the Line of Command

In many corporations there is a definite line of command or structure of designation. Trying to go to the top and bypass a person may be hazardous to your career. Know the rules of play within your company and carry out the proper procedure.

Spend Company Money Wisely

Sometimes a $50 lunch does not buy any more than a $20 lunch.

Never Use Bad Language

Using profanity shows very poor taste and can ruin a professional image.

Remember Special Occasions

Showing that you care by remembering birthdays, weddings, and births, even verbally, will enhance your image as a thoughtful executive.

Be Tidy

Keep your desk and office uncluttered. Untidiness shows lack of organization. It is unattractive and inefficient, even if you know where everything is in the piles. Form the habit of sorting your mail into folders with labels such as "To Read Later," "To Do Today," "To Do This Week."

Stand to Show Respect

When an older person or a person of senior ranking enters a group of seated people, the people should stand. The same behavior would be appropriate if a clergyman or high official enters the group — both men and women should rise.

B.

Part III
Dining

Dining

When you are a guest dining family style in someone's home, you should:

A. Reach for the dish yourself, if you want a second helping of something.

B. Ask the person closest to the dish to pass the dish to you.

C. Pass the dish clockwise.

D. Pass a gravy boat or pitcher to the next person with the handle facing him.

Answers appear on p. 92.

7
The Good Guest at the Sit-Down Dinner

Feeling at ease at the dining table is important to your sense of self-confidence. Have you ever been to a table where there were so many pieces of silverware that you didn't know where to begin? Sometimes the best connoisseurs can be thrown.

I was at a dinner party once where there were hosts at each table of eight who represented the top echelon of a corporation. We were in a foreign country and trying very hard to be sure that we understood and followed the protocol. Naturally, we Americans watched very carefully the foreign host at our table.

Soon after we were seated, a small bowl that resembled an American cup of soup was placed before us. We waited until everyone was served, and even then some time passed. Finally, the host picked up his spoon and proceeded to eat the soup which looked like the delicious French soup, *vichyssoise*. It was warm, though, rather than cold, and extremely rich and wonderful.

The host agreed with the people commenting around the room that the soup was delicious, but that its type was also a mystery to him.

As a waiter began taking away the cups, another waiter placed small bowls filled with raw mushrooms around the table. We looked at each other wondering what this was all about. Just at that moment, a waiter served the next table the soup *and* the mushrooms together. We watched as the people at the table dipped the mushrooms into the warm herb *dip* we had just devoured as *soup!* Even the host laughed and said that was a first for him.

As you can see, there are no hard and fast rules. Sometimes embarrassing things happen. We can hope that we are always served by waiters who know *when* to serve *what* and with the following guidelines, *we* will know *how* to eat what we are served!

The Invitation

• Respond to your host's invitation quickly. If you cannot give him a firm commitment at the time of his call, try to call him back on the same or second day at the latest.

• If at the last minute you find that you cannot attend, inform your host. Never send a substitute.

Take Cues from Your Host

• Watch for instructions from your host as to where to sit.

• Be especially alert when it comes to ordering. Unless you have been specifically encouraged by your host to do so, never order an expensive item. Do order foods that you enjoy, but be sure that they are similar to what the other guests are ordering. When everyone else is selecting soup and salad, don't order a luncheon steak.

• Both men and women may give their order directly to the waiter; their host does not need to order for them.

• Allow your host to deal exclusively with the waiter except when you are ordering. If you need something such as a utensil, or if you drop a napkin, or spill something, mention it quietly to your host or a nearby waiter.

• Glance at your host and adapt his method whenever in doubt as to what to do (such as how to eat chicken).

• Always watch your host and follow his cues for everything from where to sit to when it is time to leave.

• When your host offers a toast to the guest of honor, raise your glass, nod your head towards the guest of honor in affirmation of the toast, and take a sip from your glass (even if it is empty). If you wish to offer a toast, subtly request permission from your host. Never offer a toast before the host does so.

It is perfectly acceptable to make a toast with non-alcoholic beverages.

• If you are the guest of honor, you should acknowledge the toast from your host, and extend a gracious toast to him.

Never attempt to pay the bill when your host has made it clear that you are his guest. Do return the favor by inviting your host for a similar meal at some future date.

Alcoholic Beverages

Even if the host encourages the guests to order alcoholic beverages, remember that drinking mars decision-making abilities.

Today's society is very health conscious. Those people who refuse an alcoholic beverage, even if everyone else at the table has ordered one, are no longer regarded as teetotalers.

The person may not drink because of a health problem or because of personal convictions.

In today's world, standing up for your personal convictions is considered a sign of strength. People respect someone who does so. Not drinking because of personal convictions will not place you in a bad position businesswise. No one would think anything about your ordering a Perrier.*

Meal Service

• The guest of honor will be served first. The waiter will serve dishes that are intended to be passed, first to the guest of honor, then see that they are passed counterclockwise around the table.

• If the waiter serves you the food, lightly touch the dish with your left hand and serve with your right hand, unless both hands are required to take a serving. Exception: If you are left-handed do what is comfortable.

• Never be intimidated by several pieces of silverware. The utensils are arranged in the order that they will be used — use them from the outside in. The spoon and fork above the dinner plate are for dessert.

• The waiters will strive to serve all the tables at the same time and collect the plates only after all the guests have completed a course.

• Signal the waiter that you have completed the course by placing your silverware in the center of the plate.

---

*Details of alcoholic beverage service may be found in the two books listed in *References*.

• Expect the waiter to serve from the left and remove empty dishes from the right. Do not move empty dishes to the side or hand them to the waiter.

• The waiter will brush crumbs with a napkin from the table before serving the dessert course.

• If a fingerbowl with water and a slice of lemon is presented at the end of a meal, dip your fingers into the bowl and wipe your hands on your napkin below the table.

Social Graces Should Be Graceful!

• Remember that your actions are being observed. Use your very best manners at all times. Be conservative about ordering your food and beverages. Be careful with your conversation. And on top of all that, act natural!

• Table-hopping is inappropriate during a business meal.

• You should leave the table only for an essential reason such as a trip to the restroom or to take a phone call.

• Be sure to dress appropriately for the type of restaurant. Slacks and a sweater are not suitable for a formal restaurant.

• Never complain about anything, even if there is mold growing on your ice cold steak! As a guest, gratefully accept your meal rather than complain, for example, that your meat is too rare or well done.

• Loud conversations and laughter can disturb other people at the restaurant. Have a good time, but do it quietly.

8
The Good Host
at the
Sit-Down Dinner

• Visit different restaurants on your own, and choose several which conform to your entertaining needs. Frequent them regularly. When you get to know the management and staff, they will go out of their way to make your visits comfortable and enjoyable. This extra service can be a plus when entertaining guests.

• Decide on the seating arrangement before you arrive at the restaurant. (The guest of honor sits to the right of the host.)

• When you are escorted to your table, have your guests follow the maître d'hôtel: guest of honor first, then the rest of the group — first the women, then the men. However, if you have a large number of guests, you should follow the maître d'hôtel so you can conveniently see that all of your guests are seated according to your plan. It is also proper for you to offer your arm to the female guest of honor to escort her to the table. (The male guest of honor escorts the hostess.)

• Give your guests a cue regarding the courses your budget will allow. If price is not a problem, you could say, "Let's try something special today." If you need to keep the price moderate, you could mention some options on the menu within the price range you have to spend.

• Wait until your guests are served before you begin eating. In a large group, encourage your guests to eat as soon as they are served.

9
General Dining Etiquette

- It is helpful to remember that everything of importance is to the right. For example, the guest of honor sits to the right of the host, food is passed to the right.

- Take care of any special problems that may arise during the meal, such as asking for another fork if a guest drops one.

- Be a good conversationalist! Make sure each guest has a wonderful time.

- Handle paying the check gracefully. Always try to arrange that payment be handled away from the table. However, if the check is brought to you, quickly look over the charges for accuracy while continuing the conversation at hand. Use a credit card to pay the bill instead of cash.

- In a fine restaurant, thanking the waiter for refilling the water glass or serving a dish is not necessary. Your appreciation is reflected in the tip.

- Neither the host nor the guest should call attention to any accident that may occur at the table. Apologize in a few words, then later make amends.

• A man should stand when a woman leaves the table.

• In a fashionable restaurant, a woman may leave her wrap at the check room or take it into the dining room. At the table, she should let the coat drape off her shoulders onto the chair.

• When with someone who is taking you to lunch or dinner, ask what item from the menu he suggests in order to know what price range he has in mind.

• If you are having lunch dutch treat with colleagues, have someone quickly approximate each share of the bill (including the tip). Never figure the shares to the penny — that is too time-consuming and terribly gauche.

Seating

• Wait at the entrance of the room for the headwaiter to show you to the table.

• The woman or person given the most respect follows the maître d'hôtel or headwaiter.

• If taking a friend of the same sex to lunch, allow him or her to lead.

• As you face the back of your chair, enter from the left side. Leave the chair from the same side.

• A woman's escort should pull her chair out slightly.

• A woman sits on her escort's right or across from him.

• Sit with your chair several inches from the table edge.

• Sit erect. Do not slide down in the chair or crowd or inconvenience your neighbors.

• When not eating, you may rest a forearm, one elbow, or your hands and wrists on the table, but do not use the table to rest both your elbows.

• Saying grace at the table is perfectly appropriate and can be done inconspicuously.

Napkin

• After you are seated, wait to see if the waiter will unfold your napkin for you. If he does not, unfold it to a comfortable size (traditionally in half for a large napkin), and place it in your lap. (Small napkins may be unfolded completely.)

• Use the napkin occasionally throughout the meal to wipe crumbs from your mouth. Never wipe lipstick on a cloth napkin.

• If you need to leave the table during the meal, fold the napkin neatly and place it in your chair, not on the table.

• When the meal is finished, neatly place your napkin (unfolded) on the table. (Placing the napkin on the table indicates that you are ready to leave.)

Passing Food at the Table

• Food is passed in a counterclockwise direction — to the right.

• Cross the right hand in front of your body to receive the dish being passed from your left side. Change the dish to the left hand, serve yourself, then pass the dish on with the left hand. (Since most people are righthanded, passing food to the right allows for a secure grip on the dish when receiving it with the right hand.)

• Pass the salt and pepper together. Never pass them between your fingers or with your hand on top of the containers.

• Pass the cream and sugar by placing them on the table in the reach of the next person. Turn the handles toward the person for easy use. Do not pass them in midair.

• Place gravy boats or pitchers on the table so that the next person can pick them up.

Do's and Don'ts For Dining

Do's

• Do spoon the soup toward the rear of the dish. (Any drips will fall into the dish.)

• Do remove gloves before eating or drinking.

• Do cut only one bite of food at a time.

• Do soak up extra sauce with small pieces of bread. (Break off one piece at a time and lay it on the plate. After it has soaked up some of the sauce, fork it to your mouth.)

• Do break off one piece of your roll at a time and butter each piece as you eat it.

• Do break a whole slice of bread at least in half after putting it on the plate.

• Do take something distasteful or indigestible (such as gristle) from your mouth by discreetly pushing it onto a spoon or quickly taking it from your mouth with your fingers while covering your mouth with the other hand. Then lay it on your plate.

• Do put relish on the salad plate.

• Do use either the continental or American style of eating since both are appropriate.

• Do rest utensils on a plate rather than on the table when passing your plate for a second helping.

• Do dip small pieces of food into sauces served in small bowls rather than pouring the sauces over the food.

• Do take pills discreetly. Carry the pills in a small pillbox rather than in a medicine bottle. Put the pills in your hand under the table, then quickly put them in your mouth.

• Do discreetly apply lipstick at the table.

Don'ts

• Don't begin eating until the guest of honor has taken his or her first bite. Don't begin eating your dessert until everyone has been served and the guest of honor begins to eat.

• Don't put bread on the table by your plate.

• Don't use your salad plate for bread and butter. Use the bread plate on your left.

• Don't reach. Ask for items to be passed.

• Don't talk or drink with your mouth full of food.

• Don't smoke until dessert is over.

• Don't look over the rim of your beverage container while drinking.

• Don't lean over to reach your food with your face in your plate, but bring your food to your mouth.

• Don't spread jam or butter directly from the serving dish onto the roll or slice of bread. Instead, place a small portion to use on your bread and butter plate.

• Don't place your briefcase, handbag, gloves, or a stack of files on the table. (Put them on the floor out of the way of the waiter's traffic flow.)

• Don't wipe or blot lipstick on a cloth napkin.

• Don't comb or touch your hair at the table or spend much time fussing with grooming.

• Don't sprinkle salt and pepper all over your food without tasting it first. This is considered an insult to the chef.

• Don't refuse previously portioned food.

• Don't request catsup for anything other than a hamburger. It is very insulting to use this condiment on well-prepared, quality meat.

Types of Wait Persons

1. Maître d'hôtel — The headwaiter who seats you at the table.

2. Captain (American style) — Presents the menu, takes the order, and sometimes handles the wine in the absence of a sommelier (wine steward). Makes the table presentation of a flaming dessert or carving of meat.

3. Waiter (family or English style) — Brings the food and serves you.

4. Busman — Clears the table and keeps your water glass filled.

Tipping[1]

In a Modest Restaurant

Tip whoever presents the check 15 percent minimum. One tip will cover everything.

In a Fine Restaurant

Tip 15 to 20 percent of the total bill.

Tip each of the people performing the following services $1:

1. Ladies' room attendant (per woman)

2. Coatroom attendant (per coat)

3. Doorman (for calling for your car or a taxi)

4. Garage attendant (for bringing your car — $1 to $2)

---

[1]See Baldrige, p. 345.

Eating Difficult
To Manage Foods

Artichokes

1. Beginning with the outer leaves, dip the bottom third of one leaf into the melted butter or sauce, then place it with the fleshy part down between your teeth. Pull on the leaf with your fingers, scraping the meat off with your teeth.

2. Neatly pile the leaves onto the plate provided or on the side of the serving plate.

3. With a knife, cut the heart away from the bottom choke (the fuzzy center). Remove it.

4. Eat by cutting the heart into pieces and dipping each piece into the butter or sauce with your fork.

Clams and Oysters on the Half Shell
(usually served on cracked ice)

1. Rather than picking up the shell, hold the shell in place with the left hand, then with the seafood pick or fork in the right hand, lift out the entire oyster or clam.

2. Dip in seafood sauce or broth and eat in one mouthful.

Clams (steamed)

1. Clams are served in a whole shell and eaten with the fingers.

2. If the cooking did not fully open the shell, pry it open by bending it backwards with your fingers.

3. Hold the shell in the left hand, and pick out the clam with the right hand.

4. Pull out the body of the clam from the neck sheath. Discard the sheath.

5. Dip the clams into the butter or broth, then eat in one mouthful.

Lobster (boiled or broiled)

1. Lobster claws in a shell are served with a utensil that looks like a nutcracker (unless you've requested that the lobster be cracked in the kitchen).

2. Crack both large shells with the utensil, then break them further apart with your hands.

3. Hold a claw and, with the seafood fork, lift out the meat in one or two large chunks onto your plate.

4. To eat, cut off one piece at a time and dip each in the butter sauce provided.

5. With your hands, break apart the small claws, then noiselessly suck out the meat or remove it with the seafood fork.

6. With your fork, you may eat the roe and liver, both delicacies.

Shrimp Cocktail

1. Using the seafood fork, eat each shrimp if small in one mouthful. If the shrimp is large, eat it in two bites without cutting the meat.

2. When you are finished, lay the fork on the plate holding the dish.

Snails or Escargots

1. With your left hand, use the metal holders provided or your napkin to hold a shell (snails are served hot).

2. With your right hand, use the seafood pick or fork to remove the snail and eat in one mouthful.

3. You may enjoy the sauce in the shell by using the seafood fork to dip small pieces of bread into the sauce and eat.

10
Dinnerware, Glassware, and Silverware

Dinnerware

1. Dinner plate.

2. Salad plate — Placed on dinner plate if salad is the first course. Placed to the left of the forks if the salad accompanies or follows the main course.

3. Bread and butter plate — Placed above the fork.

Glassware

Arrange the stemware to the right of the water goblet in a diagonal or straight line, or in a triangle.

4. Water goblet — Place one inch above the tip of the dinner knife.

5. White wine glass.

6. Red wine glass.

7. Napkin

Sometimes at a banquet the first course is in place before the guests are seated and the napkin is to the left of the fork. At other times the napkin may be positioned on the dinner plate.

Silverware

8. Salad fork — Placed to the left of the dinner fork when the salad is served first or with the rest of the main course.

9. Dinner fork — Placed to the left of the dinner plate.

10. Seafood fork — Placed to the right of the spoon (or served with the seafood cocktail).

11. Dessert fork — Placed above the dinner plate with the prongs to the right.

12. Knife — Placed to the right of the dinner plate.

13. Butter spreader — Rests on the bread and butter plate horizontally, vertically, or diagonally.

14. Soup spoon — Placed to the right of the dinner knife.

15. Dessert spoon — Placed above the dessert fork.

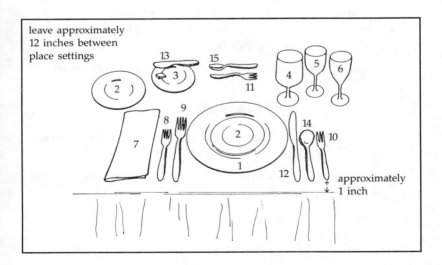

11
French Cuisine

There is no reason to feel awkward when dining in a French restaurant. If you do not know what a particular word on the menu means or what is in a particular sauce, ask. If you are uncomfortable pronouncing French words, order in English.

In a fine French restaurant, ask the maître d'hôtel what he recommends and he will describe the dishes. Because French chefs are culinary artists and modify dishes or create new ones, no two restaurants prepare their dishes exactly alike. The sauces especially vary.

Reading Menus that Contain French Terms

The word *menu* originally meant "an arranged meal" although many Americans used the word *menu* to refer to any list of food. Today both meanings are correct French.

The expression *à la carte*, meaning "list of the," refers to a list on a card of various items each of which is priced separately.

The *carte du jour*, the "card of today," is the card which lists all the items available either *à la carte* or *à prix fixe* ("at a fixed price").

The French phrase *table d'hôte* refers to the ordering of an entire meal at one price rather than ordering a meal composed of items selected from the *carte du jour*. In France, *table d'hôte* refers to the table (an entire meal purchased at a certain price) rather than to the way the meal is ordered.

A list follows of terms which commonly appear on French menus:

General Terms	Meaning
addition (ah-deece-yon)	The bill
à la (ah lah)	In the style of (or with)
amandine (ah-mawn-deen)	Made with almonds (often used with fish filets)
au buerre (oh burr)	Buttered
au jus (oh zhoo)	In its own juice
au lait (oh lay)	With milk
aux fines herbes (oh feenz airb)	With parsley, herbs, and butter
beurre noir (burr nwar)	Brown butter
brochette (broh-shet)	A skewer, or anything cooked on one
déjeuner (day-zhuh-nay)	Lunch
dîner (dee-nay)	Dinner
en croûte (awn-croot)	Baked in a pastry crust
farci (far-see)	Stuffed
frappé (frah-pay)	Chilled
maison (may-zohn)	In the style of the restaurant (also refers to recipes exclusive to that restaurant)
nature (na-tur)	Plain, in the natural state

General Terms	**Meaning**
petit déjeuner (ptee day-zhuh-nay)	Breakfast
plat du jour (plah doo zhoor)	Blue-plate (today's) special
prix fixe (pree feex)	At a set price
purée (pu-ray)	Usually means mashed potatoes
spécialité de la maison (spay-si-al-lee-tay duh la may-zohn)	specialty of a particular restaurant
sur commande (soor kuh-mawnd)	Made to your special order

Viandes (vee-awnd)	**Meats**
assiette anglaise (a-si-et awn-glehz)	Assorted cold cuts
bifteck (beef-teck)	Beef steak
bœuf (buff)	Beef
bœuf bourguignon (buff boor-ghee-nyown)	Braised beef prepared in the style of Burgundy (with small glazed onions, mushrooms and red wine)
boudin (boo-dan)	Blood sausage
canard (cah-nar)	Duck
canard à l'orange (cah-nar ah low-rawnzh)	Duck in orange sauce
carottes (cah-rot)	Carrots
cassoulet (ca-soo-lay)	Stew made with white beans and pork
cervelles (ser-vel)	Brains
châteaubriand (sha-toh-bri-awn)	Cut of beef, grilled and served with vegetables cut in strips and with a *béarnaise* sauce
coq au vin (coke oh van)	Chicken in a red wine sauce with mushrooms, garlic, small onions, and diced pork

Viandes (vee-awnd)	Meats
côte de bœuf grillée (coht duh buff gree-yay)	Grilled beef rib
côte de veau (coht duh voh)	Veal chop
côtelette (coh-tlet)	Chop
croque-madame (croak mah-dom)	Grilled chicken and Swiss cheese sandwich
croque-monsieur (croak muh-syeuh)	Ham and Swiss cheese sandwich, fried
daube (dohb)	Chunks of meat stewed with vegetables
dinde (dand)	Turkey
entrecôte (awn-truh-coat)	Translates as "between the ribs" and refers to steak cut from between two ribs of beef, usually grilled or fried
entrecôte marchand de vin (awn-truh-coat mar-shawn duh van)	Steak cooked with red wine and shallots
escalopes de veau (es-cah-lop duh voh)	Thin, boneless steaks
escalopes de veau cordon bleu (es-cah-lop duh voh kor-dohn bluh)	Thin slices of boneless veal with ham and cheese
faisan (fay-zawn)	Pheasant
filet de bœuf (fee-lay duh buff)	Tenderloin
filet mignon (fee-lay meen-yohn)	Tender beef filet with sauce
foie (fwah)	Liver
gigot d'agneau (zhi-goh dahn-yoh)	Leg of lamb
jambon (zahm-bown)	Ham
lapin (lah-pan)	Rabbit
lard (lahr)	Bacon

Viandes (vee-awnd)   Meats

pâté de foie gras (pah-tay duh fwah grah)	Paste of goose livers
porc (pohr)	Pork
pot-au-feu (poh-toh-fuh)	French version of boiled beef dinner
poulet (poo-lay)	Chicken
ris de veau (ree duh voh)	Sweetbreads of veal
rognons (rohn-yown)	Kidneys
rôti de bœuf (roh-tee duh buff)	Roast beef
saucisson (soh-see-sown)	Large sausage; sliced for serving
steak tartare (stehk tar-tar)	Uncooked ground meat seasoned with salt and pepper and served with a raw egg yolk on top and sometimes with capers and parsley on the side
tournedos (toor-nuh-doh)	Small slice of beef, round and thick, from the heart of the filet of beef; sauteed or grilled
veau (voh)	Veal
venaison (vuh-nay-zown)	Venison (deer, wild bear, any hoofed animal)
volaille (voh-lye)	Fowl

Poissons (pwah-sown)   Fish

homard (oh-mar)	Lobster
bouillabaise (boo-yah-behz)	Fish chowder from French Riviera; made with fish, olive oil, tomatoes, and saffron with water or bouillon oysters
huitres (wee-tr)	Oysters
coquillages (co-key-yazh)	Shellfish
coquille St. Jacques (co-key-yuh san zhahk)	Scallops

Poissons (pwah-sown)	**Fish**
crevettes (cruh-vet)	Shrimp
cuisses de grenouille (kwees duh gruh-noo-yuh)	Frogs' legs
ecrevisse (ai-kruh-viss)	Crawfish
escargots (es-kar-goh)	Snails
fruits de mer (frwee duh mair)	Seafood
truite (trweet)	Trout

Légumes/Fruits (leh-gyum/frwee)	**Vegetables/Fruits**
ananas (ah-nah-nah)	Pineapple
artichauts (ar-tee-show)	Artichokes
asperges (as-pairzh)	Asparagus
aubergine (oh-bair-zheen)	Eggplant
avocat (ah-voh-kah)	Avocado
champignons (shom-peen-yown)	Mushrooms
citron (see-trowhn)	Lemon
cœur d'artichauts (kur dar-tee-show)	Artichoke hearts
compote de fruits (kom-poht duh frwee)	Stewed, mixed fruits (fresh or dried), served cold
cornichon (kor-nee-shown)	Type of small pickle
courgette (koor-zheht)	Zucchini
crudités (crew-dee-tay)	Raw vegetables served as an appetizer
épinards (ai-pee-nar)	Spinach
fraises (frehz)	Strawberries
framboises (from-bwahz)	Raspberries

Legumes/Fruits (leh-gyum/frwee)	Vegetables/Fruits
frites (freet)	French fries
haricots (ah-ree-koh)	Beans
haricots verts (ah-ree-koh vair)	Green beans
laitue (lay-tu)	Lettuce
oignon (uhn-yown)	Onion
pêche (pehsh)	Peach
petits pois (ptee pwah)	Green peas
pomme (pohm)	Apple
riz (rhee)	Rice

Sauces (sohs)	Sauces
béarnaise (bair-nehz)	Brown sauce made with butter, mayonnaise, vinegar and egg yolks
béchamel (bay-shah-mel)	Made with butter, milk, and parsley
bordelaise (bor-duh-lehz)	Made with red or white wine, bone marrow, herbs, beef stock
hollandaise (oh-lawn-dehz)	Heavy sauce made with egg yolk, butter, and lemon
madere (mah-dair)	Brown sauce made with Madeira wine

Desserts (day-sair)	Desserts
biscuits or *petits gâteaux (bee-sqwee) (ptee gah-toh)*	Cookies
bombe glacée (bowm glah-say)	Ice cream "bomb"
bonbon (bohn-bohn)	Candy
café glacée (kah-fay glah-say)	Ice cream with coffee flavoring
crème brûlée (krehm brew-lay)	A rich dessert pudding made with vanilla and cream, which is lightly coated with sugar, placed under a broiler, and then cooled for two to three hours before serving '

Desserts (day-sair)   Desserts

gâteau (gah-toh)	Cake
glace (glahs)	Ice cream or sherbet (iced)
mousse (moos)	Whipped (fluffy) ice cream, custard, or pudding
pâtisserie (pah-tees-uh-ree)	Pastry
petit-beurre (ptee-burr)	Butter cookie
tarte (tahrt)	Pie

Divers (dee-vair)   Miscellaneous

ail (ai-yuh)	Garlic
anchois (awn-shwah)	Anchovy
consommé (kon-soh-may)	Enriched, concentrated, clarified meat stock
crème Chantilly (krem shawn-tee-yee)	Whipped cream
fromage (froh-mahzh)	Cheese
lait (lay)	Milk
œuf (uhf)	Egg
pain (pan)	Bread
petit pain (ptee pan)	Roll
poivre (pwah-vr)	Pepper
potage (poh-tahzh)	Soup, usually with cream base
sel (sehl)	Salt
sucre (sue-kr)	Sugar
thé (tay)	Tea

Many of the definitions listed on pp. 86-92 of this book are taken from *Executive Etiquette*, by Marjabelle Young Stewart and Marian G. Faux, pp. 94-104.

B, D.

Part IV
Entertainment
Planning

Entertainment Planning

When is it a good time to entertain clients with a party?

A. Anytime is appropriate since everyone likes a party.

B. Only on weekends.

C. When you have a budget that has been set aside to cover these expenses.

D. When you can meet certain objectives by having this kind of party.

E. When there is time set aside for the commitment in giving it and the staff to see that it is done well.

Answers appear on p. 110.

12
Planning the Corporate Party

The days of the unlimited expense account are no longer the norm. Corporations are cutting back in every financial area. For this reason, they are watching more closely the business person's expense account. Highly visible business entertainment, weekend getaways, and inclusion of family and friends are no longer common.

When done correctly, entertaining is one of the most productive tools available to the business person. Billions of dollars are spent each year for entertaining to create additional business for the company. Business entertaining is not just fun — it is profitable. Cost effectiveness of entertaining *is* a consideration.

Reasons for Entertaining

1. To form relationships which will lead toward further business between two companies.

2. To express gratitude. Treating someone to an expensive formal dinner or even a simple lunch is a good way of saying, "Thank you."

3. To celebrate a business success. Reward yourself and others for a job well done.

4. To help make decisions. Sometimes getting away from the office atmosphere allows people to think more openly and objectively when a difficult decision needs to be made.

The Key Ingredient

Careful planning is the key ingredient to successful entertaining. There are so many details that it is important to write everything down.

Make sure you have remembered to arrange every detail as well as to remember what details you have arranged! Your written plans can be a valuable resource when you analyze the success of your business entertaining and plan future events, whether large or small. In planning a party consider: business objectives, cost, and time commitment.

Tips for the Good Host

Being considerate of your guests is the most important prerequisite for any host or hostess.

Mary, who entertains frequently with her executive husband, has learned to plan events and allow enough time for people's relaxation as well. Packing an agenda full of entertaining is not relaxing or fun without including personal time for them to do what they choose.

There are certain how-to's that apply to every situation in which you will entertain:

• Select a location for the event which will be comfortable for the guests. The area should be cool and well ventilated. Music should be pleasant and soft.

• Plan the arrangement of the buffet table and beverage service areas, and the seating and reception line to facilitate the movement of guests.

• See that adequate serving utensils, napkins, and other service items are available.

• Consult with your caterer to determine the types and amount of beverages to serve for the length of the party and the tastes of your guests.

• Select tablecloths, napkins, floral arrangements, and serving pieces that are interesting. Arrange dishes, utensils, and serving pieces artfully on the table.

• Use as many flowers as your budget will allow. A good florist will help you enhance the table decor.

The Always Rules

• Treat every guest as a VIP (very important person).

• Always ask if your guests would like to participate in a certain activity you have planned.

• Plan events that you know your guests will enjoy. For example, some guests may prefer a Western barbecue to a formal sit-down dinner.

• Be sure there is sufficient room and plenty of chairs.

• Offer a variety of beverages.

• If you notice that a guest is not touching some of his food, ask him if he would like more of the items that he has eaten. Never put your guest on the spot by asking him why he has not eaten something.

• Food, beverages, service, and entertainment should be top quality.

• To cut down on expenses, invite fewer guests, select less-expensive foods, or serve fewer courses — *never* sacrifice quality.

Be a gracious host! Smile. Mingle with your guests. Visit with everyone. Introduce newcomers and see that shy guests are put at ease.

• In your home, provide the restrooms with guest towels, fancy soaps, and other special items.

• Never make an issue of something that went wrong in front of your guests.

• Make sure that your dishes, utensils, and serving pieces sparkle.

• All service personnel should be impeccably groomed. Uniforms should be spotless and pressed. Hair and nails must be well manicured.

Menu Planning

Because food is the most important component of a successful formal meal, the menu should be planned with great care.

The number of courses you serve is dependent upon the importance of the occasion and the size of your budget. Naturally, for very important affairs, prepare the most elaborate meal you can afford. A formal luncheon should consist of two to three courses and a formal dinner, of three to seven courses.

Two to Seven Course Meals

Two Course Meal
1. Salad, vegetable, meat
2. Dessert

Three Course
1. Appetizer or soup
2. Salad, vegetable, meat
3. Dessert

Four Course
1. Appetizer or soup
2. Salad
3. Vegetable, meat
4. Dessert

100

Five Course
1. Appetizer
2. Soup
3. Salad
4. Vegetable, meat
5. Dessert

Six Course
1. Appetizer
2. Soup
3. Fish
4. Vegetable, meat
5. Green salad and cheese
6. Dessert

Seven Course
1. Appetizer
2. Soup
3. Fish
4. Sorbet
5. Vegetable, meat
6. Green salad and cheese
7. Dessert

• Make sure your menu is suitable for your guests' appetites and tastes, the type of event, and the time of day and year. Serve hearty, hot dishes in the winter and light, cool ones in the summer. Never serve finger food and dainties to a group of men or *steak tartare* to a group of women.

• Select foods within your budget. Berries out of season should not be added. If you need to watch your budget, select easily attainable foods.

• The food must awaken the taste buds and please the eye.

• Select as many fresh foods as possible.

• Plan nutritious meals. Avoid fried or heavily sauced foods.

• Select foods with a variety of tastes, colors, textures, and temperatures.

• Since many people are controlling serious health problems with special diets, the wise host should ask his guests if they have any special dietary restrictions. This can be conveniently done when extending invitations or receiving RSVP's by telephone.

Guests to Invite

1. Keep a guest list on file.

Include: name, address, phone numbers, profession, company, special interests, and type of guest. Also record invitations extended (acceptances and regrets) and other notes.

Types of guests

My associate, Sally, has an interesting code of reference she uses when designating the types of guests:

SE   Senior executive

KE   Key employee

CP   Company professional (such as an accountant, attorney, or banker)

IC   Important customer or client

PC   Potential customer or client

CL   Community leader

GO   Government official

M   Media

ST   Special talents (such as an artist, musician, writer, sportsman, educator, or scientist)

2. Choose guests wisely.

Select a variety of personalities and business types.

Consider their role in relation to yours in achieving your business objectives.

Consider those with a balance of special interests and talents.

3. Extend invitations in plenty of time.

Determine the Seating Arrangement

• By rank.

The diagram below displays a basic seating arrangement.[1]

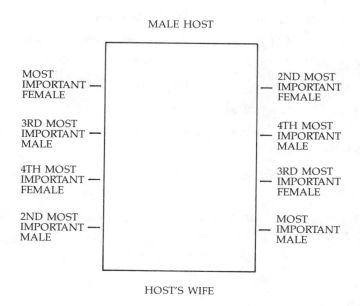

<hr />

[1]Letitia Baldrige, *Complete Guide to Executive Manners*, p. 307.

Many details are taken into consideration when ranking guests. A seat of honor should be given to:[2]

Someone of official rank.

A foreign guest.

Someone who is visiting you.

Someone who is elderly.

A person who has had a distinguished career.

Someone who formerly held an appointed or elected office or military rank.

Someone who is celebrating his birthday, an anniversary, a promotion, etc.

• By personality to encourage interesting conversations.

Be sure that guests who are seated together do not have major differences of opinion or personal conflicts.

1. Seat guests with common interests together.

2. Seat quiet or shy guests next to outgoing ones.

3. Seat a guest between someone his own age and someone older.

4. Seat men next to women.

5. Do not seat husbands and wives next to one another. If there is more than one table, husbands and wives should sit at different tables.

_____

[2]*Ibid.*, p. 308.

13
Types of
Entertaining

Breakfast

An effective breakfast meeting at a conveniently located restaurant can extend the productivity of your day. The meeting should last between 45 minutes and one hour.

Lunch

Meeting over a one to two-hour long lunch to discuss business is another way to extend the productivity of your day. Traditionally, it is the time to form and strengthen personal relationships that could lead back to substantial business.

Dinner

Business dinners should be reserved for special occasions when you really want to please someone. Choose the nicest restaurant you can afford and plan for an enjoyable, leisurely meal.

You should always invite your guest's spouse. However, this is not necessary when you are working and dinner becomes an extension of your productive workday.

At Home

If you are the lady of the house (either the company executive hosting the party or the wife of the executive), you have the responsibility of seeing that every detail involved in entertaining at home is handled to perfection. You may plan the party yourself or delegate that responsibility to someone in the company.

You must see that every aspect of this event in your home is arranged to be sure that the event is especially memorable. (See "The Corporate Wife" in the section "Relationships in Business.")

Keep the following points in mind:

• If necessary, enclose a good map and directions to your home with the invitation.

• Make every effort to see that each guest who comes into your home has a wonderful time.

• Be sure your home is attractively decorated and that the space is arranged for a good flow of people in conversation.

• If necessary to keep small children from being underfoot, hire a baby-sitter.

• Decorate with lots of fresh flowers to make your home look especially festive.

• Make sure there is plenty of comfortable seating for your guests including tables and chairs for sitting to eat.

• Place plenty of ashtrays and coasters throughout the house.

• Hire an excellent caterer and make sure there is plenty of well-trained help.

• Set an attractive table. (Do not use plastic placemats and paper napkins.)

• Plan a delicious (although not necessarily elaborate) meal for your guests.

• Have beverages on hand that you know your guests will enjoy.

• For large crowds, use car valets.

• For large parties, appoint several people from the company to act as co-hosts. They will help greet guests as they arrive, introduce guests to each other, and bring newcomers into conversations. A co-host should be seated at each table to help with conversation and see to any special needs of the guests at his table.

The Informal Stand-Up Party or Formal Buffet

A popular and easy way to entertain large groups of people is through an informal stand-up party featuring snacks and beverages. This type of party takes the least amount of time and usually costs less than other large events. It can be held at your office, in your home, at a restaurant, or at a hotel.

The more formal buffet is an excellent way to give a large party for a special reason, such as to celebrate an exceptionally successful business year. It is scheduled between 6:00 and 9:00 P.M. and lasts between two and three hours.

Reception

The reception, a formal event, is given only for very special events, such as to celebrate the company's silver anniversary, to honor a retiring senior executive, or for the opening night of the symphony.

It may be held either between 6:00 and 8:00 P.M. or 10:30 P.M. and midnight.

Entertainment
Cost Effectiveness Checklist
For One Client

1. Name of client _____.
   Title _____.
   Company _____.

2. Type of entertainment.
   Breakfast _____.
   Lunch _____.
   Dinner _____.

3. Length of meeting _____.

4. Business objectives for the meeting.
   _____.
   _____.
   _____.

5. Business objectives completed.
   _____.
   _____.
   _____.

6. Cost of dining _____.

7. Revenue generated from meeting.
   _____.

Entertainment
Cost Effectiveness Checklist
For a Party

1. Attendance.
   Number of people invited _____.
   Number who attended _____.
   Number of RSVP's _____.
   Number of no-shows _____.

2. Cost.
   Budget for party _____.
   Amount actually spent _____.

3. Vendors used.

	Good (+) / Poor (−)	
_____	_____	_____ .
_____	_____	_____ .
_____	_____	_____ .

4. Planning.
   Beginning date _____.
   Ending date (of event)_____.
   Total hours spent on project _____.

5. Business continued or generated.
   Actual continual business with _____ (number of guests).
   New business generated with _____ (number of guests).

6. Thank you notes received _____.

7. Results.

   _____ .
   _____ .
   _____ .

Tips for the Good Guest

• Respond quickly to the invitation. Always RSVP within one week. Your host must have an accurate response to order the proper amount of food and beverages.

• If you cannot attend the party at the last minute, call your host the next day to apologize. Never earn the reputation of a "no-show."

• Arrive promptly. Leave at the appointed close of the party.

• Always remain standing until your host indicates where he wants you to sit.

• Mingle and visit with many different people, not just those you know. Avoid monopolizing anyone's attention.

• Accept refreshments even if you do not eat or drink them.

• Assume food served without silverware (such as wedding cake) is finger food.

• Balance your drink (wrapped in a napkin) and your plate of hors d'oeuvres in your left hand. Keep your right hand free for eating and shaking hands.

• Put a coaster under your glass when setting it on a table.

• Enjoy your host's food and beverages, but be careful not to eat or drink more than your share.

• If you are on a special diet, you should either mention it at the time you accept the invitation or decide you will eat what you can without mentioning it unless your host asks you about it. Enjoy the foods you can eat. Push the other foods around a bit with your fork. Probably no one will notice what you did or did not eat.

• Be sensitive as to whether smoking is appropriate.

• Master the art of formal dining — everyone *should*.

C, D, E.

Part V
Interviews, Appointments, Introductions

Interviews, Appointments, Introductions

If you find yourself running late for an appointment, you should:

A. Stop and call the person you are meeting to let him know.

B. Hurry as fast as you can to get there.

C. Don't worry — the other person is probably late, too.

D. Call the person and ask if he would like to reschedule due to your being late.

E. Call the person and tell him you just can't make it — you are running late.

Answers appear on p. 138.

14
Interviews

If you approach job hunting in the right way, it can be a pleasant experience and you can make a game of it. If you know the rules of the game and how to play successfully, you will not have any reason for feeling afraid. Your attitude does make a difference.

When applying for a job, remember that you are there to make a contribution to that company. Be prepared in every way to make the best possible first impression, then relax. All interviewers have been on the other side where you are, and most of them are caring people. However, they probably interview several people during a day, so be prepared to give them the best *you* the first time you meet.

Here are some guidelines to follow.

Preparation

1. Learn everything you can about the available position and/or the company where you are applying. Ahead of time, ask for any information about what the company expects from an employee and how the job is structured. With this

information, you will be able to ask pertinent and intelligent questions and impress upon the interviewer that you are aggressively seeking the position and know what it is about. You will impress any interviewer with this kind of preparation.

2. Talk with someone who works for the company you are considering. Sometimes an insider's viewpoint of day-to-day activities and description of company morale is helpful.

A young woman who accepted a job with a good opportunity for advancement (or so she thought) was later disappointed to learn that the politics of the office had caused low employee morale. Advancement was based on who people knew rather than on job qualifications. She wished she had spoken with a friend within the company before the interview and could have been more informed of such inside problems.

3. Prepare a well-written resume and carry copies with you. Include in the resume all you can pertaining to your job-related activities and accomplishments.

List references on a separate sheet. Before you use the people as references, ask them if they mind being called. You will find that most people are delighted to be considered reputable and pleased to help with your job search. Your friends and business associates can be your best sources and will be flattered when asked to help.

Always appear in control of your destiny and never desperate. Remain professional; not panicked to get a job. The right offer may come when you least expect it.

4. If using a recruiting firm, be sure to check its credentials and lists of clients. You may want to call a few of these clients to see how thorough the agency was in helping them find the right job.

Finding a job "fit" between a person and a position takes tact, finesse, and an appreciation for long-lasting relationships. The long-term credibility of the search firm is important in placing you where you will be able to use your talents to full capacity.

5. Make an appointment with the decision maker. If you are in sales, contact the vice-president of Sales and Marketing. If you are an executive, contact the president or an executive as high up as makes sense. Just as is done when making a sales call, go to the top when possible. The executive looking for a top-paying position should avoid the personnel office. But if the boss insists you begin there, you have no alternative.

Dress for the Interview

1. Be comfortable with what you wear. A new pair of shoes or new clothing that is uncomfortable will tend to make you feel and look uncomfortable.

2. Know the dress code of the company and look like you already work there. If you are applying at a very conservative company, you should not show up in designer high-fashion clothing.

3. In most cases it is safe for both men and women to wear a business suit which is always appropriate. Wearing minimal jewelry is advisable. Professional make-up for daytime and conservative hairstyle is appropriate. Executive women do not look like they are ready for an evening on the town with lots of jewelry and too much make-up.

4. Avoid extremes of any kind. You want to make the very best first impression you possibly can. It *is* a fact that you will be judged on the way you present yourself visually before you ever say a word.

5. Immaculate grooming is extremely important. A man once told me that the first thing he noticed was hands. Nails

should be well-manicured and clean. Fingernails that are bright red and too long do not look businesslike. Shoes should be polished; clothes should be crisp and clean. Too much cologne is offensive.

6. It is not the cost, but the *quality* of your clothing that is extremely important. People who hire executives notice investment dressing, so wear something of natural fibers — such as wool, silk, or cotton — and dress appropriately for the position you want to have, not for the one you have now. Dress as the boss, and you will become one!

Men

1. Suit patterns could be solid, pinstripe, or chalkstripe. Colors are best in navy, or gray (medium to dark) with a white shirt and conservative rep or foulard tie.

2. A well-shaven look is better than a beard. Facial hair can detract, even if you have grown it proudly and keep it neat. If you have a moustache, it should be crisp and clean — not shabby or too long over the sides of your mouth.

3. Bracelets or necklaces have no place in the corporate interview. A simple wedding ring or watch is fine, but not little finger rings with large stones.

4. Starched shirts, well-polished shoes, and clean fingernails are a must. Be sure your briefcase and wallet are of good-quality leather. Never carry your wallet in your back hip pocket — only in your coat pocket. Take off your suit jacket any time you are driving to keep the shape neat and pressed. It is important to wear over-the-calf socks with lace or slip-on business shoes — no loafers or boots.

Women

1. Suits could be navy, burgundy, gray, or beige. Wear a blouse that is a business style — no frills or low cuts. Your

skirt should be well enough below the knee that when you sit, it does not rise above your knees.

2. Jewelry should be minimal. Too much can be distracting. Eye contact, not your bracelet, is important.

3. Hairstyle should be businesslike, not stringy or shaggy.

4. Make-up should enhance and not detract. False eyelashes went out of style years ago.

5. Hosiery should be taupe, natural or sheer navy, gray, or ivory.

6. Accessories should be of quality leather. Shoes should match your suit in color or intensity of color. Carry either a briefcase *or* purse, but not both. Take notes with a gold or silver pen.

Both Men and Women

Strive to be as well-prepared and comfortable as possible. Try on everything you will wear ahead of time so you will not feel stiff and appear nervous. You want to appear as confident and relaxed as possible. When you *know* you look good, you will *feel* good, and that will be communicated in an interview.

Etiquette of the Interview

1. Behave as professionally with the secretary and/or receptionist as you would with the interviewer. The secretary may well turn out to be a good friend and her opinion may be very important.

2. Arrive about fifteen minutes early to catch your breath and tidy up. Do not use this time to catch up on work or make telephone calls.

One interviewer told me when he went out to the reception area, he found the applicant on the telephone. The applicant had to finish his conversation before going in to be interviewed. He ruined his business impression even before he had a chance to talk to the interviewer.

3. Give the secretary your appointment time and name.

4. Walk confidently with good, straight posture. Extend your hand when you meet someone.

5. Wait to be seated until the interviewer indicates where you are to sit.

6. Do not smoke or chew gum under any circumstances. Doing either of these things will hinder your speaking effectiveness. You need to be as articulate as possible.

7. Always call the interviewer by his proper name. Never use the first name unless the person is a close friend.

8. Put your materials on the floor next to you or in your lap. Never invade the interviewer's personal territory by placing anything on his desk.

9. Be ready to *listen* and absorb what is being said. Take directions from the interviewer's body language. Smile or nod occasionally to hold his attention. Maintain good eye contact throughout the interview. Ask important questions that pertain to the job. This is *not* the time to ask about vacation time or raises.

10. Remain confident, but not cocky. Be yourself. The point you want to make with the interviewer is that you have the qualifications for the position and desire to do a good job for the company.

11. When leaving, shake hands again. It is appropriate to ask when you can call again or when you can expect a decision.

12. Sending a short, businesslike follow-up thank you note will make a good impression. Thank the interviewer for taking the time to meet with you. End by saying that you are looking forward to hearing from him.

13. When the final interview takes place and you are negotiating for salary and benefits, remain confident and ask for the salary range you feel you will need. Your bargaining power at this point is in your favor since the company wants to hire you. Be specific about salary and other financial options you will need.

14. If there is a business reason for benefits such as a country club membership, you may ask about them. But do not ask if you simply like to play tennis or work out. Most of the time, the employer will mention options such as these without you having to ask about them.

When You Are the Interviewer

Remember how it felt when you were being interviewed, and do everything you can to make the applicant feel at ease. Having good manners during an interview reflects directly on your company.

1. Show respect for the person you are interviewing by smiling and treating him as the valuable person he is. Never put yourself in such a superior position that you put down the applicant either verbally or non-verbally.

2. Let the applicant know by telephone or letter whether he is being considered for the job.

Mary interviewed for a job she really wanted. The interview went well and she felt that she had the job. But instead, the personnel manager quit returning her calls and seemed to always be out. Finally, after several weeks, he sent a letter informing her that she did not get the job without an explanation.

Mary debated whether to call and tell him that she felt she had been treated unfairly, go above him to his supervisor, or simply ignore her hurt feelings and look for another job. After much consideration, she decided to quit expending energy in anger, and move on to better opportunities.

In the following months, Mary was surprised when she began receiving sales referrals from the personnel manager. He was telling people that they would probably enjoy working with her. Mary's decision to let go her hurt feelings turned the situation into a positive one. The relationship remained intact for future business opportunities. Think about the concern you may be causing an applicant to feel by not informing him of your decision to hire or not hire him, and notify him quickly.

3. Keep any information you discuss during the interview confidential. Be honest about the opportunity. If you know the person is not right for the job, tell him. Do not let him dangle, hoping for the job. This is not fair to him and shows lack of caring on your part.

15
Performance Appraisals

Most companies today offer what can be a very fine tool in assessing strengths and helping you grow through and overcome your weaknesses. It is called a job evaluation or appraisal. When a manager gives an appraisal and an employee receives one in a positive manner, the benefits are great.

Giving an Appraisal

1. Evaluating someone is not always easy. Take enough time to think through clearly how to give the individual the best information in a positive way.

2. Articulate clearly what you want to say without demotivating the person. Always remain positive and in control.

3. Concentrate on the person's strengths.

4. Feel confident that you can give an accurate appraisal by:

• Being completely familiar with the job responsibility you are appraising.

• Being sure that the employee knows his priorities. Giving guidance with accountability is important. The employee's priorities are not necessarily those of the supervisor. He will not know what is expected of him unless he is told.

• Maintaining enough communication with the employee to give guidance, and waiting to give an appraisal until you have known him long enough to assess whether he is carrying out his duties in the way you prescribed.

I heard of an employee who appeared to be doing a good job. He was turning in the assigned work on time and often took the initiative to do more than what was required. But his work was inaccurate.

The problem was discovered when errors started showing up in other departments that were caused by the employee's mistakes. If the manager had followed through and checked his employee's work, in a performance appraisal he could have shown the employee an area which needed improvement and saved the company a number of costly mistakes.

Receiving an Appraisal

1. Realize that an appraisal should be a motivating tool. It is not a report card. You do not have to get straight A's. An appraisal is simply an instrument to keep you on target — a road map. An appraisal evaluates where you are to see if you are headed in the right direction for where you are going. It helps you grow and assess how you are doing.

2. Listen attentively to each comment and take notes of what is being said.

3. Wait until the appraisal is finished so that you have an overview before you start asking questions.

4. If there are points that you feel were mishandled or misinterpreted in the appraisal, take time to discuss them then, or ask if you can see your supervisor later.

5. Always remain positive through an appraisal and show gratitude both for positives and negatives being pointed out.

6. Rather than taking the negatives personally, look at them objectively. Grow from any negatives. Learn from your mistakes. Turn those failures into opportunities.

16
Appointments

Making the Appointment

The first encounter you usually have in a business transaction is making the appointment by telephone to meet your client or business associate. Here are some points to keep in mind:

1. Before calling, list the points you want to cover including:

- Who you are.

- With what company and product you are associated.

- Why you are calling.

- Questions to ask to find out if there is a need for your company service or product.

- Several appointment times to offer as options should the person be interested in your product.

2. Make cold phone calls between 9:00 A.M. and 4:00 P.M. The beginning and end of the day are difficult for most executives.

3. Call when *you* can concentrate on the conversation without interruptions or incoming calls.

4. Do not address the client by his first name. Understanding deference — giving respect to whom it is due — is important.

A person who has worked into a position of authority has earned the right to be addressed as "Mr.," "Mrs.," or "Ms." The client will tell you if it is all right to call him by his first name.

5. Be brief. Leave the details to be discussed in person. Only tell enough to create an interest, but not give the whole sales pitch before you meet.

6. To gain the person's attention and interest, show a smile in your voice by speaking clearly and enthusiastically.

7. Listen to what the other person has to say. Let him do 80 percent of the talking.

8. Take notes of his wants and needs. (Also see Chapter 4, "Telephone Techniques.")

At the Appointment

The tact and poise you use when you first meet your client is extremely important. From the minute you meet the secretary, you need to make the best first impression. To represent your company well, you must project professionalism not only through your dress, but also through your manners.

1. Greet the receptionist or secretary with a smile. Give her your business card, and tell her whom you are meeting.

Do not interrupt the secretary's work with idle conversation, but be friendly and courteous. Speak with her just long enough to build a rapport. She may be the best friend you have. If several people call on her boss within a given day, she will remember and comment about you if you have shown her respect and courtesy. She will also remember you if you have not shown her respect.

2. Do not ask to use anyone's telephone or ask anyone's secretary to run an errand.

3. Arrive about 15 minutes early to assure that you have time to gather your thoughts.

4. If after about 20 minutes you have not been called to meet your appointment, decide how important the meeting is and if you should continue to wait. Ask the receptionist or secretary to remind the individual that you are waiting. After 30 minutes, you may want to tell the receptionist that you can no longer wait and request another appointment.

5. Greet the client with a smile and a handshake. Maintaining good eye contact is extremely important. Not looking at a person can reveal fear, lack of self-confidence, or give the impression of hiding something. Your body language messages, visual poise (posture), and appearance all contribute to a positive or negative first impression. Your executive presence is at stake.

6. Whether you are on a sales call or meeting with a senior executive in your own company, wait to be shown where to sit. Move quickly to the designated seat and say, "Thank you."

If you are not told where to sit, wait for the executive to sit first, then sit directly across from him. (This goes for both men and women.)

7. Put all your presentation materials (and purse) on the floor, not on the desk. Keep only a note pad and pen on your lap. If you need a great deal of room to lay

out your materials, request in advance that your meeting be held in a conference room (or you could ask the client to come to your office).

8. Do not request refreshments if none are served.

9. Let the client do most of the talking the first time you meet. Many sales are lost because the salesman does too much of the talking. Remember, you do not learn anything when *you* are talking, only when you are listening.

10. Take notes.

Two competitive companies were making sales calls on the head of a corporation. When the first company's representatives called, they did not carry with them any paper to take notes. When the second company's representatives called, each carried a portfolio briefcase with a writing pad in a leather cover.

At the end of the day, the executive said to the second pair of men, "It's obvious to me that you've come with serious intentions. You each came prepared to take notes of what I say.

"The first company's salesmen came without note paper. It was obvious that they weren't interested enough in our business to write down what I said, so I'm giving the business to you."

Taking notes projected the representatives' professionalism and showed that they were interested in serving the company as well as possible. The attention you pay to details can make the difference between a successful and unsuccessful sales call.

11. Keep your comments brief and your time short. Respect the client's time and come back later if you need more.

12. When you leave, thank your client for his time, leave your card, and shake hands, maintaining good eye contact.

13. Thank the secretary or receptionist as you leave.

Sales Calls on Top Management

1. First, feel good about yourself.

2. Then feel good about your product and your company.

3. Earn the right to meet with the top management. If you present yourself in a positive manner and feel positive about yourself and your company, then you are more likely to feel on the same level as your client. If you do not make that assumption, he never will. The manner you assume will transcend his attitude. You must conduct yourself as being on his level.

4. Familiarize yourself with the business on which you are calling. Learn something about the industry, size of the company, and other details.

5. Do your homework. Analyze the company's financial statement, its annual report. If you do not know how to do it, read "How to Analyze an Annual Report" by Merrill Lynch. From analyzing the report, you will learn the company's key direction and the management team's long-term goals.

If the reports are privately held, you will have to obtain the financial information by making initial calls on one of the company's middle managers.

6. The whole purpose of the first meeting is fact-finding and to arrange for a second meeting.

7. Outline the purpose of the call. Come prepared with four or five questions. The client will appreciate your directness because it will lead you to a faster conclusion. No top-level executive wants to feel you are wasting his time (or that he is wasting yours).

8. Always leave the head of the company feeling as though he has gained something from the call other than

just meeting you. Do not use the first call for rapport building — you should only talk about the fish on the wall for so long!

The Client's Role

1. You (both male and female executives alike) should stand, step out from behind your desk, and shake hands with the person calling on you.

2. Give the salesman a warm smile and make good eye contact. This says you are expecting him and are ready for the meeting.

3. Indicate where you would like the person to sit. I once called on a very nice person, an owner of a large firm, who had an impressive, large office. He escorted me into his office, but left me standing there a good five minutes while he made some "last minute" calls he said were very important.

In front of his desk were two chairs, and over to the side was a setting with a couch, two large chairs, and a table. I wandered around the room looking at the pictures and plaques on the wall, waiting to know whether he intended for me to sit very formally at his desk or in the more informal area with the couch and table for presenting materials. It became awkward for me to remain standing, so I seated myself on the couch and looked through magazines while he finished the conversations.

He was truly a delightful executive, yet had no idea that he had left me so rudely standing all that time. Your *awareness* of how to treat the guest is important to the guest.

4. If you have to rush the meeting, apologize to the salesman, and reschedule. Remember, you were once in a position of having to call on executives. It is frustrating to prepare information only to feel rushed when you do not have the amount of time for which you had planned.

5. Ask your secretary to hold or screen calls for you when you have someone in your office to discuss business. Nothing can cause lack of concentration more than being constantly interrupted by phone calls, then having to refocus on the discussion each time.

6. When the meeting is ended, shake hands, and escort the person at least to the door of your office.

17
Introductions

There is nothing more important to you than your name. It is sweet music to your ears. Why? Because it is the most personal thing you own.

The most important thing to remember about introductions is to *make* them. A person would rather have you tell him that you forgot his name and ask for it than to stand in a group of people and not be introduced.

Forgetting names happens to everyone at some time. I once forgot the name of a boyfriend whom I had been dating for three years. I went absolutely blank. (I blamed it on love.) The conversation kept going until I finally remembered his name. I acted as if I had just started the conversation and introduced him to a friend.

You might have heard of the person who forgot someone's name and thought he would be very clever by asking how to spell it. He was mortified when the person said, "S-M-I-T-H." Honesty is the best policy — admit your forgetfulness and ask.

On the other side of the fence, if you realize someone is struggling with *your* name — quickly come to the rescue and tell your name. My last name is so difficult that I immediately offer it either by pronouncing or spelling it. I can usually see the person having to introduce me almost sigh in relief.

Guidelines to Showing Deference

The basic rule to remember is that the person you mention *first* is the one you are honoring.

1. A man is presented to a woman. "Mrs. Brown, this is Mr. Smith." An exception to this rule is usually made in business when a woman employee is introduced to an important executive of the firm. In such situations, respect is shown to the executive by mentioning him first. "Mr. Gilbert, this is our new receptionist, Ann Burns."

2. When you are introducing members of the same sex, the guiding factors are age and rank or degree of distinction. Again, the person to be honored is mentioned first.

3. Present the younger to the older person. "Mr. Elder, may I introduce Mr. Young."

4. Present the lower in rank to the higher. "Mr. Allen [vice-president of your firm], this is Mr. Adams [a junior executive]."

5. Present a less distinguished person to a more celebrated person. "Miss Celebrity, may I present Miss Jones."

6. Present a layman to a clergyman. "Reverend Stocks, Mr. Glenn."

7. Present others to your parents. "Mother and Dad, this is my friend, Carol Wells." The only exception would be some very distinguished person, such as a president of a large corporation.

8. When two people of the same sex are approximately the same age, rank, and prominence, it does not matter who is mentioned first.

Other Tips

1. In all social introductions, mention something about the person being introduced so that when you leave, the group has a starting point for their conversation.

2. In a dining situation, you should introduce yourself to those sitting next to you if you have not been introduced previously.

3. Men should rise to meet a woman when possible. Women should rise for a much older man or woman or a person of distinction. When you are unsure about when to rise, go ahead and do so.

4. At a social function, a married woman who has kept her maiden name should *clearly* introduce her husband with *his* last name emphasized. Mary Braggs should say, "This is my husband, Jim *Paxton*."

This will keep other employees from referring to him as "Mr. Braggs." When introducing them, you would say, "This is Mary Braggs and her husband Jim *Paxton*."

5. If you realize you have named the wrong person first, say, "I'd like to introduce you to . . . ." For instance, if you are introducing your new employee to the boss, you *should* say, "Mr. Jones, I'd like you to meet Bill Harris, our new

employee." But if instead you began on the wrong track with, "Bill . . . ." finish by saying, "Bill, I'd like to introduce you *to* Mr. Jones. Mr. Jones, this is Bill Harris, our new employee."

6. In answering an introduction, the simplest reply is, "I'm glad to meet you," or "How do you do?"

Remembering Names

To remember someone's name, practice saying it several times during your conversation with him.

Recently, I met a young woman who was an expert in remembering names. During our conversation, Vicki often repeated my name. I found myself really liking her. Not only did she make me feel she was truly interested in me because she kept saying my name, but I also knew she was practicing saying it, looking at me in the face and remembering it. She was being gracious, but repeating the name of someone whom she just met was a habit she had developed to remember names.

Once when my family had moved to a new city and we were visiting a church, the minister asked our names that first Sunday. The next Sunday, he called us by name.

Those people in highly visible positions usually become experts in remembering names. They know that people are flattered and impressed when their names are remembered.

In the hospitality industry, doormen are smart to remember the names of traveling business people who often stay at that hotel. People show their appreciation in being remembered through tipping generously.

Another way to remember names is to visualize something which will remind you of the name. For example, you could remember Mike Barnes' name by picturing a microphone standing in the middle of a barn.

A, D.

Part VI
Meetings

Meetings

How can you be most prepared to attend a meeting?

A.   Get a good night's rest.

B.   Assume that paper and pencil will be supplied at the meeting.

C.   Study the agenda or program ahead of time.

D.   Consider what objectives you have for attending the meeting.

Answers appear on p. 162.

Introduction

The professional uses good manners when attending meetings and keeps in mind the question "What is the most gracious thing to do?" when organizing them.

We have all attended dull meetings. But we need to ask ourselves how we would feel if we were the speaker and looked out on the audience to see people snoozing away or slumped in their seats with their arms crossed over their chests.

We as meeting participants who have organized meetings are well aware of the effort that goes into the preparation. We need to be considerate of the speaker and give him the courtesy of looking alert and listening attentively.

Any of us who have chaired meetings know how important it is to feel that we have accomplished something by holding the meeting and that the participants have appreciated our efforts.

As a young executive, you may spend as much as 40 percent of your time in meetings. With so much of your time devoted to meetings, you must make sure that the time is well spent. Whether your role is participant or meeting chairman, it is crucial that you project your professionalism through your behavior during these meetings — it is important that you know how to conduct yourself in the eyes of your peers.

In this section, you will find some guidelines to follow which will help you show that you are professional and project the positive attitude which keeps you professional.

18
Qualities
of a Good Participant

As a participant, you are just as responsible for a successful meeting as the meeting chairman.

1. Go to the meeting prepared to contribute in order to maximize your meeting time.

• Study the agenda if it is available before the meeting.

• If an agenda is not distributed ahead of time, find out what items will be discussed.

• Think through how the topics relate to you and your job. Decide what information you need to gather from the presentation.

• Prepare your comments in advance and prepare documents to support these comments.

• Bring needed materials.

2. Arrive on time or several minutes early.

3. Come with a positive attitude, ready to learn.

4. Before the meeting, introduce yourself to those you do not know, especially to those sitting next to you.

5. Watch for cues where to sit.

• Do not sit next to the meeting chairman unless asked.

• Choose a seat where you will be comfortable.

• If you will need to leave early, sit next to the exit door.

• If you have a physical problem such as difficulty hearing or seeing from a distance, sit close to the front so that you can give your full attention to what is being said.

6. A smoker should choose a seat where he can be the most considerate of others (next to a door or open window).

• To decide if smoking is appropriate in the meeting:

Look to see if there are ashtrays on the table.

Watch to see if the executive in charge of the meeting smokes.

Ask the people sitting next to you if they mind you smoking.

7. If you have a choice, drink soda from a glass rather than a can or bottle.

8. If you are to make a presentation, be sure you have rehearsed it well. Before the meeting, check to see that all audiovisual equipment is working.

9. Always ask permission before using a tape recorder.

10. Bring a note pad and carefully take notes.

11. Act and look alert and interested.

• Give the speaker your full attention. Do not talk or doodle. Both are distracting to the speaker and other participants.

• Sit up straight in your chair.

• Keep eye contact with the speaker and give positive feedback such as a smile or a nod.

• Do not interrupt the person speaking. If you want to make a comment, write a note to yourself and bring up your point at break or after the meeting is adjourned.

• Do not begin or become involved in a conversation with people around you if the subject is not pertinent to the discussion.

12. Control your emotions if you disagree with something being said. Do not shake your head to show that you disagree. Present your negative thoughts later in a positive way.

13. Make only relevant comments.

• If you are a new executive with the company, keep in mind that you may feel more comfortable feeling your way at first. You may want to wait until you have been with the company a little longer to feel secure about making a number of suggestions in a meeting.

• If you can see that your comments are not being accepted, discuss the situation later with your supervisor. It is much better to be in disagreement one to one than it is one to fifty.

14. Do not point out anyone's shortcomings publicly.

15. If you are asked to take some action before the next meeting, be sure to do so. Follow through. Come prepared to report the results at the next meeting.

16. Make a note of the meeting chairman's criticism of your and others' ideas.

17. Thank the meeting chairman as you leave.

Taking Blame

Sometimes people ask me what they should do if blame is placed on them in a meeting for something that they did not do. The person placing the blame may be doing it indirectly or unintentionally. Not wanting to appear defensive or lay blame on someone else, people usually say nothing to explain the truth of the matter.

I think you should always stand up for what is truth. But to do that, you do not need to react by saying, "That's not the way it happened at all," or "That's not right," or "I did not do that." If what was said needs to be clarified in the meeting, you might say, "Excuse me, but I think I might be able to give you some insight into this situation of which you might be unaware."

If what was said was not relevant to the topic being discussed, but you want to set the record straight to the chairman, which you should do, approach him outside of the meeting. Say, "Excuse me, Mr. Jones, but something came up during the meeting that I would like to clarify with you. Do you have a few minutes or could I take some of your time later in the day?" Then explain the situation to him, relating the facts.

19
Qualities of a
Good Meeting Chairman

A chairman's planning, organization, and behavior is just as critical to the success of a meeting as is his following the correct rules of order when conducting a meeting. There are a number of reasons why the chairman must plan carefully. First, corporate direction is affected by the decisions made during meetings.

Second, meetings are probably one of the biggest expenses of a corporation. By carefully planning and monitoring, the chairman can insure that the meetings remain productive. This will help counteract the cost of the multiplied hourly wages of the participants.

Third, the chairman's careful planning will help eliminate mistakes. Especially during large meetings, mistakes made are highly visible to hundreds of people.

Fourth, the chairman must carefully plan in order to project the correct corporate image.

In local meetings, the managers should be careful to project the national company image. A manager who communicates an image that is inconsistent with the national one causes confusion.

I know of a company which held an elaborate, formal banquet at the end of a two-day convention to honor a group of outstanding salesmen. The salesmen and their wives thoroughly enjoyed the dinner. But the manager chose as after dinner entertainment a comedian/singer whose routine was risque.

The people with taste were very offended to think that the company would expect them to enjoy that type of entertainment. That manager's decision severely damaged the corporate image in the eyes of the salesmen and, especially, their wives. Some of those salesmen eventually left the company because of the incident.

Surprisingly, this sort of thing often happens. If the manager had followed the rule of doing the most gracious thing, he would never have chosen that off-color entertainment and offended some of the company's most valuable employees. Eventually, the manager was fired.

In his planning, the chairman must strike a balance. He should keep in mind that the business objectives must be reached, but that the meeting must also be interesting.

One company became so well known for its boring national meetings that its employees quit attending. The company started inviting speakers not so technically oriented who still spoke on topics pertaining to business, but with a lighter presentation. The employees began going again to the meetings.

The time and energy the chairman spends preparing for a meeting is well worth the effort. Here are some things to keep in mind when planning a meeting:

1.   Plan to cover only major topics of priority. Allow enough time for interaction to complete the meeting's objectives.

2. Hold only necessary meetings. For example, do not hold weekly department meetings if there is no real reason for one every week.

3. Schedule meetings in the morning when people are fresh and alert. Never schedule meetings for Friday afternoons or just before a holiday.

4. Decide who should attend the meetings.

• Invite the people well ahead of time — at least two weeks in advance if out-of-town people are involved.

• Make sure the people know that the meeting is required.

5. Choose the right atmosphere for the meeting.

• Make sure the room is at a comfortable temperature and the lighting is good.

• Provide ice water. You may want to have paper and pencils available.

• To keep participants awake and alert in a long meeting, take a break at least every hour and a half.

6. Give the participants an agenda well before the meeting to inform them of what subjects will be discussed.

• Be sure the agenda describes the purpose, what is to be achieved, and what is to be prepared by the participants to achieve this.

• If the participants need to read information before the meeting can begin, distribute the information in advance so that meeting time is not spent just reading.

7. Always start the meeting on time.

• Cover important agenda items first. Although you will have allowed a certain amount of time for each topic, some items may take longer than you expect.

• Closely follow the agenda and keep the meeting on track.

8.   If the participants do not know each other, introduce them by name and title. It is important that everyone understands the others' areas of responsibility.

9.   Be sensitive to non-smokers. If possible, designate a separate seating area for smokers.

10. Stay in control of the meeting.

• As chairman, you should establish the agenda topics and allow for discussion.

• Make sure that all questions raised are answered.

• You must manage any conflict between participants and still achieve the meeting's goals.

11. Summarize decisions reached and give assignments for follow-through.

• It is your responsibility to be sure each participant knows what actions are required. Otherwise, everyone will leave thinking, "Great meeting; we accomplished a lot," then at the next meeting, wonder why nothing was accomplished since the last meeting.

12. Give credit to those people who helped with the meeting, either in giving a presentation or in preparing materials.

The Master of Ceremonies

There may be a time when you are asked to serve as master of ceremonies. Here are some guidelines to follow:

Before the Event

1. Even if someone has excellent credentials, do not assume that he is a good speaker.

I was told of a situation in which a woman with a number of degrees was chosen to speak at a particular meeting. The master of ceremonies gave her a glowing introduction. But the woman turned out to be the worst speaker the people had ever heard. The master of ceremonies had placed her on a high pedestal based on her portfolio she sent.

You or someone in your organization whose opinion you trust should try to hear the speaker before inviting him. If you cannot hear him in person, ask that he send a tape.

2. Notify each participant of the meeting's time and place and what each person will be expected to do. Suggest type of dress.

3. Prepare the room to meet the needs of the speaker. Provide microphones, podium lighting, audiovisual equipment, and a glass of water.

Opening the Meeting

1. Gain the audience's attention, open the program with a welcome, and introduce yourself.

2. Ask the designated person to give the invocation if one is desired.

• Ask the audience to rise, and introduce the person giving the invocation. After he finishes, ask the audience to be seated.

• Tell the audience to enjoy the meal and that you will be talking with them again later.

3. After the meal, regain the attention of the audience. With a few remarks, introduce the speaker.

Introducing the Speaker

An executive was asked to address a class of graduating college students in a city about 100 miles away. He knew no one there and wondered why he had been chosen.

The night of the address, the dean of students began his introduction, "Mr. Smith does not know it, but about a year ago I was in his community and heard a talk he was giving to a group of businessmen. The talk was so fine, I decided this was the man we wanted to speak to our next graduating class." For the next five minutes he gave a fully accurate and complete outline of the talk of the previous year.

The waiting speaker grew more pale with each flattering word. Little did anyone know that the address he had in his pocket was the talk so carefully outlined to the waiting audience.

Whenever introducing a speaker, be sure to abide by the following guidelines:

1. Write the speaker's office and request suggestions for the introduction. Ask questions about his background, about what he does for a living — not about the details of his speech.

2. Highlight the part of the person's background that best relates to the group.

3. Pronounce the speaker's name correctly.

4. Be enthusiastic.

5. Relate personal facts about the speaker. Tell about his family or humorous situations he has been in that will not embarrass him.

6. Highlight key points the speaker wants the group to know, but do not give away the talk the speaker has prepared or steal his opening lines.

7. Be genuine. Do not overemphasize the speaker's qualifications or overpraise.

8. Do not draw attention to negative conditions such as a poor microphone, a warm room, or the speaker's ill health.

9. Be brief.

While introducing the guest speaker to a group of bankers, the master of ceremonies listed the speaker's virtues in glowing terms.

"That introduction," grinned the guest, "reminds me of the man who on judgment day stuck his head out of the grave and read the epitaph on his headstone.

" 'Either somebody is a terrible liar,' " he said, " 'or I'm in the wrong hole.' "

Closing the Meeting

1. After the speaker finishes, shake his hand, and thank him enthusiastically over the microphone. Your actions will usually cause the audience to applaud.

2. Signal to the audience that it is time to leave by thanking them, then walking away from the microphone.

3. End the program on time. To insure that this will happen, tell each speaker his time limit before the program begins. If he runs over, signal to him to cut his speech short.

4. Throughout the meeting, be sure to smile and keep your face relaxed, no matter what happens.

Taking Care of a Speaker

1. During your first conversation with the speaker, let him know what fee you plan to pay him. Keep in mind that a speaker's time is his commodity. His time is commensurate with earnings — a product which he sells.

In considering the fee, you must take into account the hours it takes the speaker to prepare and the time he spends arriving and leaving. For a two-hour speech, the speaker actually spends four hours or half a day. For one day's speech, the speaker may need to stay overnight one or two nights, spending a day and a half to two days. People who have never spoken themselves do not realize how much time is involved.

2. Follow up by sending the speaker a proper invitation in which you state the date and name of the event, the time of day he will speak, the amount of time he will have, the time of day you would like him to arrive, and the topic of the speech.

Do's

1. If the speaker will need to be up before room service is operational, be sure to make breakfast arrangements the next morning if necessary.

2. Arrange the speaker's schedule so that he will have some privacy before his speech. Talking to a number of people would be tiring to him and his voice.

Don'ts

1. Don't take the speaker home from the airport to meet the family. He will probably be tired and want to check into his hotel immediately.

2. Don't keep him out late the night before his appearance.

3. Don't ask him a lot of gossipy, personal questions.

4. Don't give him a club memento after he speaks. He would rather have a thank you letter and copies of any newspaper clippings on his speech.

20
Guidelines
for a Speaker

Accepting the Invitation

1. Acknowledge the invitation immediately.

If declining, rather than saying, "I can't do it," give a good reason. If you do not, you will lose your credibility.

In declining, say that you would be happy to try to comply at another time.

Remember that if you cancel at the last minute, you are putting the person who asked you to speak on the spot.

2. Be considerate by making a firm commitment.

One time I was asked to speak one year in advance, but not told until a couple of weeks before the event what time of day I would be speaking. This was frustrating because I could not prepare very well until I knew the time of day I would speak. The entire day's program could not be scheduled any sooner because one of the speakers, a big-name person, could not decide when to arrive. Everyone was inconvenienced because of that person's lack of consideration.

3. Ask which of the topics you speak on would best fit the needs of the audience.

Send an outline of what you will be covering (not the entire speech) to be approved. By doing that, there will be no misunderstanding when you arrive of the subject matter of your talk. In business, communication can make you or break you. Do not leave any room for misunderstanding.

4. Send an outline for an introduction even if it is not requested.

5. Ask how long a time you will have to speak, and what types of people will be in your audience — sex, titles or positions, and ages.

6. Find out when on the program you will appear, whom you will follow, and what time of day you will speak. Once when I spoke at a sales convention, I found out that I would be following two speakers whose topics were technically oriented — very dry subjects. I knew that the audience would need a break, so I prepared my presentation to be light and fun.

If you are scheduled to speak after lunch, you had better be funny! Otherwise, the people might have trouble staying awake!

7. Find out in advance the details of your physical arrangements such as your flight and hotel.

8. Clarify the fee in advance.

Unless you can afford the time and the risk of paying for your trip and accommodations yourself, during your first conversation with the people asking you to speak, you need to discuss whether a fee will or will not be paid to you. As a prerequisite ask, "What arrangements do you have for a fee, and what could I expect?"

Unfortunately, when discussing the fee, you can never assume anything. I have mistakenly assumed too many times that I would be paid immediately after I finished speaking. Often, I waited weeks, sometimes months, for my fee to be paid.

A minister's wife told me that one time her husband was asked to perform a wedding out of town. Her husband agreed and, *assuming* that he would be reimbursed (as he should have been) for the expenses of the trip, he never discussed an honorarium. He and his wife took the time out of their schedules and drove.

The minister never received one penny, not even for his expenses. It was an awkward situation which he did not know how to handle.

If you plan to speak for free, but expect your expenses to be paid, accept the offer to speak by saying, "I would be happy to come. My only prerequisite is that my expenses must be met."

A speaker needs to have the privilege of saying, "No, I can't come if you can't pay expenses." It might work out that receiving payment for his expenses might not be necessary if he were planning to be in town at that time anyway.

The key is to discuss the matter of payment in the beginning to prevent any possibility of misunderstanding later. A speaker should not hesitate to talk about fees, because he has a job to do and has a right to know in advance what fee will be paid.

Dress for a Speaker

1. For a formal evening affair, a woman speaker should wear a long or very dressy short evening dress, not party pajamas or evening pants. In the daytime, she may wear a dress, a softly tailored outfit, or a business suit, depending on the type of audience.

2. For daytime affairs, a man should wear a conservative suit — not a sports jacket, open-necked shirt, or sweater.

3. If a company meeting is being held in a resort area and after the seminar everyone will go golfing, a man could wear golf slacks and a sports shirt and a woman could wear a casual dress.

4. For evening affairs, a man should wear a black dinner jacket (not colored), with or without a black evening vest. Colored cummerbunds are usually distracting. White unruffled dinner shirts are preferred.

Preparation

1. If you have handout materials — such as tapes, books, and handout sheets to be displayed on a table — make sure that they arrive ahead of you. It is the job of the people hosting you to decide where to place your materials and have them ready. Otherwise, you would need to arrive in time to lay them out.

Sending your materials ahead instead of packing them in your luggage is a precautionary measure. If your luggage is lost, you will still have your material available at the meeting.

2. See the room setup and check the equipment the night before you are scheduled to speak, if possible. Once when I was speaking for a national convention, I went to check the room the night before. I tested my slides to see how well they would project on the screen. Thank goodness

I did, because all of my slides projected backwards! The equipment had been set up for rear screen projection, which means that the image is reversed. Had I shown up the next morning and put on my carousel without checking the equipment, my whole presentation would have been ruined.

3. Arrive early. If you are a speaker in the afternoon, you may want to attend the morning session as a participant to get the feel of the type people and subjects being taught. In your speech you will be able to refer to comments made in the morning session.

4. Ahead of time it is a good idea to learn everything you can about the company and the individuals within that company so that you can personalize your talk with specifics. Find out the names of people who have been successful in some way and what they accomplished. For example, if you are talking about success, you can give the people in that company credit for their successes. You could say, "Mary knows about success. She successfully quit smoking." "Joe knows about success. He's just been promoted."

5. If you have to cough or sneeze while speaking, simply turn away holding a handkerchief or tissue to your face with your back to the audience. Apologize, say what you can to put the audience back at ease, and begin again.

After the Speech

1. If possible, stay around for at least an hour. People in the audience like to ask questions and make comments. It is rude to be so busy that you have to leave right away to catch the plane for your next speech.

2. As soon as you return home, write acknowledgments and thank you notes to everyone involved. Doing that takes such little time and effort and not many people do it. It means so much.

A speaker I met last year is especially gracious. I participated in a seminar he taught only because I was scheduled to be speaking later for the company that held it. The company had told me that he was an excellent speaker and had invited me to attend.

At the break I introduced myself and explained why I was attending the meeting. He greeted me and asked for my card. Shortly after that, I received a letter from him. He said, "It was so nice to meet you — a fellow speaker — and to have you participate at the seminar I held. I hope our paths cross again sometime."

They did cross again in a Dallas restaurant. I was having breakfast at the table next to him and recognized him. After greeting him, I told him where we had met before. He graciously responded, then again asked for my card. Within a few days, I received a package from him. It was his newest book.

Sending me the book was not just a professional touch, but something he did to show he cared. You can imagine what kind of fine reputation he has because of the way he treats people. Just concentrate on being gracious. You can always achieve your objectives at another meeting. (For additional information see the comments on sit-down dining in the section "Dining.")

A, C, D.

Part VII
Relationships
in Business

Relationships
in Business

What should I do to best get along with my peers?

A. Entertain them socially as often as possible.

B. Be a team player.

C. Respect others' work time rather than burdening them with personal talk.

D. Respect others' personal space — desk, work area, typewriter, etc.

Answers appear on p. 186.

21
Male/Female
Relationships

Today one of the most common concerns among men is, "How am I supposed to treat a woman who is now my business equal?" and for women, "Should I expect the traditional female courtesies when I am an executive?"

Because women have been achieving high levels of success, the role of the female has changed. No longer is she employed only as a secretary, but also as a boss and peer. This puts a whole new code of conduct into effect among the office staff as to how to treat women in the day-to-day activities at work.

You as a woman can and should set the stage for how you *want* to be treated. If you expect equal pay and equal status on the job, you should also expect to be treated as an equal in other areas. For instance, a woman should be willing to open a door first if she arrives there before a man whether it is during or after work hours. However, if a man and woman arrive at the door at the same time, the man still opens the door. A woman should realize that a man often enjoys holding the door for her, and she can non-verbally indicate to him whether he should.

This mutual admiration society approach within the office can lessen the strain of doing something just because you are female.

In today's business world, the male/female relationships at work tend to be looked upon as those of colleagues, not as sex-oriented. This works well as long as both the man and woman feel comfortable in letting go of some previous manners taught, such as the woman expecting the man to help her with her coat or to always open the door for her. (Today a female employee can open the door for a senior executive unless he moves forward to open it for her.) Common sense should be used when it comes to such issues.

Handling Sexual Advances

This seems to be a problem not only with men approaching women, but with aggressive women approaching men. A good rule of thumb is to not give *any* suggestion of interest when an overture is obvious. It *does* take two to start any relationship.

Such things as a lingering eye contact or a handshake held too long can give cues without a word being said. If someone makes eye contact and lingers with a smile, simply look away and break that eye contact. If a man shakes hands and continues to "hold" hands, just take one step back. Your hand must follow and it will break the handshake.

If you are actually approached verbally, try reacting with humor rather than making an issue. Talking about your spouse or current date can discourage an attraction.

The important thing to remember is that relationships can begin very innocently with kind remarks and invitations to lunch or dinner.

Here are some professional ethics to keep in mind:

• Never accept advances of any kind from a married person.

• Dating clients is dangerous and unprofessional unless the business relationship has come to an end and the social part of the relationship can be free from interfering with business.

• Dating the boss is awkward and inappropriate.

Male Customer's Compliments and Advances

As far as handling a male client's compliments, a simple "thank you" is all that is necessary. Handling advances can be done two ways — with humor or by ignoring them. Always remain gracious and professional and do not give any non-verbal clues of being interested.

In addition, try thinking of yourself as a professional who happens to be a woman rather than a woman who is trying to be professional. You will find that as you put this into practice, your response to these situations will be natural and effective without being offensive or unfeminine.

Refusing a Lunch Invitation

Refusing a luncheon with someone is your perogative, whether in or outside of business. If you truly feel that a man has ulterior motives in asking you to lunch, you can simply state that you would prefer meeting at your office where your information is more readily available.

When you feel hesitant about going to lunch with a male client for this reason, it is probably better in the long run not to give any opportunity for misunderstood intentions. Keeping everything within business hours and the business setting is always appropriate.

22
The Role of the Female

Addressing the Female Peer

There are several names that should *not* be used by a man or another woman in referring to or addressing a woman: "girl," "dear," and "honey" are just a few.

Once when giving a presentation to a group of women, the speaker referred to them as "girls." Nothing was said at the time, but later she received a phone call from one of the women who had attended.

The attendee said, "If you don't mind my making a suggestion, don't ever call women 'girls.' It's demeaning. I have other friends in the business world who also dislike it. We're not girls — we're women." I have heard many comments from women executives that they just do not like being called "girls" under any circumstances.

If a man seems to be acting condescendingly toward you by calling you "honey," consider the man's attitude before you react. Some men have formed this habit long ago, see nothing wrong with it, and do not mean any disrespect by it. In this case, "honey" does not reflect how the man feels about you professionally. However, if you feel that the man is being condescending, do one of the following:

- Ignore what he said.

- Say, "My name is _____."

- Revert to calling him Mr._____.

- Continue the business conversation and stick to facts.

Female/Female Relationships

The old idiom "It's lonely at the top" is true. Within any organization, there are defined levels. You cannot fully participate in two levels at the same time. You are either in management or on the support staff. You have to make a choice. You cannot maintain your identity at one level if you associate more comfortably and more obviously on another level. In other words, you cannot maintain a professional distance and be "one of the daily lunch group."

Many women in support roles have levels of informal power in the company. A secretary or receptionist can control whether you talk to her boss on the phone or get an appointment with him, she can relay your messages in a negative or positive manner, or she can fail to notify you of an important meeting. If you develop a good business relationship with her, she can pass on valuable tips to help you deal with her boss.

When dealing with a female who is in a lower position than you:

- Don't act condescendingly or demeaningly toward her.

- Don't patronize her or preach to her on how she should try for a more important position.

• Never confide any of your personal problems or matters to her and try to avoid learning any intimate details of her personal life. Keep all such conversations at a superficial level.

Wives of Male Associates

The wives may be concerned with potential intimate situations especially during out-of-town trips. Female business associates are sharing something with their husbands that wives cannot share in — his work. Keep this in mind whenever you are around the wives. Always be friendly and treat them with courtesy.

Entertaining a Male Client

A woman entertaining a male client can create an awkward situation unless she sets the mood and arranges the meeting appropriately. Some men may still be uncomfortable with women initiating the invitation. Here are a few suggestions to make things go smoothly for both parties:

1. When calling the man, make sure you tell him clearly that you would like to take him to lunch to discuss business. Say something like this, "Bob, I'd like to take you to lunch and we can discuss this further." Or make the request in a neutral way by asking the client to let your company treat him to lunch. The woman executive is then seen as an agent of the company and not as a woman asking a man to lunch.

2. It is preferable to choose a restaurant you go to often, ideally a club where your company owns a membership, and arrange ahead of time for the bill not to be brought to the table. Make the reservation in your name, and give the restaurant your credit card number ahead of time. Quickly excuse yourself during dessert and coffee to sign the check, or sign on the way out.

3. If you go to a restaurant where the bill must be brought to the table, simply quietly ask the waiter to have the check brought to you. Use a credit card to pay it. If the man insists on paying, it is best to let him, rather than make an issue of who should pay. If lunch meetings are frequent, you may want to alternate paying. (Incidentally, after signing a credit card receipt, pull off both carbons. This will eliminate any possibility of figure changes which might be made after you leave.)

4. Tipping should be added to include the usual 15 percent and perhaps an extra $1 or $2 if the headwaiter has been extra helpful.

5. If your colleague orders a cocktail, never feel you will offend him by ordering a Perrier or other non-alcoholic beverage. If you do not drink because of personal convictions, you should never feel second best because you choose not to drink.

Lunching with Other Women Employees

Decide ahead of time who will be in charge of the bill and pay the person your portion plus the tip when the bill arrives. Be very careful to do this quickly and generously. There is nothing more irritating to a waiter and to other women who are in a hurry to get back to work than to have to wait impatiently while someone tries to figure a portion of the bill to the penny.

Taking Another Woman to Lunch

If as a woman you call to ask another woman to have lunch with you, you should intend to pay the bill.

Be especially gracious in ordering as the guest of an entrepreneur. Remember, a business owner is *not* on a corporate account. Be respectful that prices may affect her company profit in a different way. (Incidentally, no matter what company your client is with, always order a moderately priced item unless he or she specifically suggests something expensive. Expense accounts are well monitored these days.)

The Corporate Wife

Leigh and her husband were planning to go to a reception of another company in order to get to know the people for business purposes. It was a very important occasion. My friend's husband was out of town and, due to bad weather, could not fly home in time to go to the reception.

Leigh certainly did not want to go without him, yet even without being able to talk to him about the situation, she knew that meeting the people at that reception was important to him. Leigh decided she would go alone. She chose an outfit that was conservative, but appropriate, and went.

At the reception, she introduced herself and explained that even though her husband had been detained, she had wanted to come alone to meet the people.

Making this special effort was one of the nicest things Leigh could have done for her husband. He asked her all kinds of questions about whom she had met and what the people were like. Also, the other company people were impressed to realize that the man's wife was so special. This woman knew what to do to support her husband in the way he needed it.

Behind a successful man is often a loving and supportive woman. Your role as your husband's support becomes more important the farther up the ladder of success he climbs. But how can you feel comfortable entertaining his clients and/or business colleagues? Here are some guidelines in the art of entertaining for you to follow and be a gracious hostess always:

• When planning to entertain and you feel a need for assistance from your husband's staff, ask your husband whom to contact and what responsibilities can be shared with you.

• Familiarize yourself with the business your husband is in and be able to speak the language when around his colleagues and clients. If he is in the high-tech industry, you should know the difference between hardware and software; in real estate, know something about the general market and interest rates; in advertising, understand market share, prime time, and layouts.

• Stay well read and knowledgeable about what is going on in your country, your city, and internationally.

• Stay informed of the latest fashions and continually upgrade your image to go along with his. Be sure you wear clothes that are currently in style and are appropriate to the occasion. Update your hairstyle and make-up periodically. Always reflect the best image you can for your husband's sake and yours.

• Celebrate his successes with a surprise candlelight dinner just for you two or an unannounced weekend getaway.

• Stay in good physical shape and get plenty of rest.

Mary, a very dear and special friend, is the epitome of a successful corporate wife. I asked her what she thought was the most important thing she does for her husband. She said, "I try to remember I'm not just a support to my husband, but rather I'm part of a team."

Mary has learned that his success becomes *their* success and together they share the reward.

23
Employer/Employee Interaction

J. C. Penny said, "When task becomes more important than the person, business is lost. Business is friendship."

It is important not to become so involved in the work at hand that you think of it as having more value than the people with whom you work!

Qualities of a Good Manager

1. Treats employees as worthy contributors who have the ability to make valid contributions when asked.

2. Looks for positive qualities to commend rather than only dwelling on mistakes made.

3. Tries to help the person who made a mistake understand how to do a better job the next time, rather than making him feel stupid and like a failure.

4. Knows when to relax and have a good time when tension builds with deadlines.

5. Shows appreciation when extra effort is given by an employee.

6. Watches for growth in employees and for opportunities to help the employees advance in the company.

7. Surrounds himself with the best, knowing that quality employees make him look good, rather than surrounding himself with inferior people, thinking that this will make him stand out more.

8. Is sensitive to personal problems and supportive.

9. Maintains authority and control within the office.

10. Gives constant guidance so that all employees fully understand what is expected of them.

11. Keeps communication within the office open and flowing. This builds morale when people feel they know what is going on daily.

12. Holds meetings regularly enough to air problems, set goals, or discuss business, but not just for the sake of holding meetings.

13. Tries to draw out the talents of the employees as they fit into the work situation.

14. Sends thank you notes and condolences to employees.

15. Answers his phone calls or has his secretary answer them on a timely basis.

16. Sets the standards of excellence in the office by *his* attitude and the way he treats people, knowing that those people will in turn treat other employees the same.

17. Knows how to develop his people to their full potential.

18. Is able to delegate responsibility when necessary and not hang on to trivial duties.

19. Deserves respect by being a person of high integrity.

20. Does not expect *too* much of an employee, but remembers that the employee has other priorities besides his job.

21. Always expresses confidence in an employee in the presence of a client, then later privately discusses with the employee any problem brought to his attention by the client.

The Prayer of a Boss

"Dear Lord, please help me —

"To accept human beings as they are —

"Not yearn for perfect creatures;

"To recognize ability and encourage it;

"To understand shortcomings — and make allowances for them;

"To work patiently for improvement — and not expect too much too quickly;

"To appreciate what people do right — not just criticize what they do wrong;

"To be slow to anger and hard to discourage;

"To have the hide of an elephant and the patience of Job;

"In short, Lord, please help me be a better boss!"[1]

Qualities of a Good Employee

"Give the world the best that you have and the best will come back to you."

Madeline Bridges[2]

---

[1] John Luther, "A Supervisor's Prayer," *Bits & Pieces,* F/No. 41, p. 24.

[2] *On the Upbeat,* 15 Mar. 1985, p. 1.

1. Always maintains professionalism within the work hours by being on time and working when it is time to work, playing when it is time to play, and not mixing the two.

2. Learns all he can about his job responsibility and the company for which he works.

3. *Never gossips* to other employees — gossip *always* gets back to hurt someone.

4. Tries to keep personal problems from interfering during work hours. Does not use production time to burden another employee with ongoing problems.

5. Respects other employees' personal space and does not violate it. Does not sit in another's chair, on his desk, or pick up things off his desk. He realizes that work space is like a home away from home and should be respected as such.

6. Keeps the office tidy on an individual basis.

7. When asked to attend a meeting, knows whether he should make comments or only listen. Does not offer opinions unless asked, but *is* prepared in case he *is* asked.

8. Appreciates seminars paid for by the company as much as if he had paid for them himself.

9. Offers to give extra effort when he sees it is needed. His willingness to work later and harder will be remembered when promotion time comes.

10. Shows leadership qualities when the opportunity arises.

11. Is always truthful.

12. Respects company time. Takes breaks and lunch hours on a timely basis.

Qualities of a Good Secretary

A separate section of this book is given to the secretary because she is so important to her boss in today's work place.

She is (or should be) his extension and as such reflects his personality and integrity.

A sale was lost by a secretary when an important client called the office trying to talk to "Mr. Big" about his business. Mr. Big happened to be a very personable and likeable person, but his secretary had let her position go to her head and tried to be overly authoritative to the point of being rude. When the call came in, she overscreened the client as if to say, "I'll decide if you are worthy enough for me to put you through."

The client never had a chance to do business with that company nor meet Mr. Big. He took his large amount of business to another company.

A good secretary:

1. Becomes the extension of her boss that he or she *intends* her to be. She reflects her boss's personality and way of doing business.

2. Is supportive at all times.

3. Understands completely the decision-making activities under her boss's control. Whenever she is in doubt about how to handle something, she asks what to do.

4. Is ready and willing to listen actively or passively when her boss needs to use her as a sounding board.

5. Keeps secrets. A loyal and closed-mouthed secretary is indispensible.

6. Is willing to do little things at a moment's notice that may seem "beneath her" (such as running out to buy her boss a sandwich if he is working late).

7. Sharpens her people skills. She is the sensitive link to the public and to other employees.

8. Gives the best first impression over the phone or in person, always sounding and looking her best.

9. Is cooperative with all the departments and their employees. She knows that she is also in the public relations business.

10. Stays organized and helps her boss stay organized.

11. Knows the functions of each department within the company and is ready to channel people to whatever department can help them.

12. Stays gracious with complaint calls. A secretary often takes the brunt of angry customers who want to complain to the boss. She remains gracious with a smile on her face even when she does not feel like it.

13. Keeps a positive attitude. She is the Mom of the office. We all know that the attitude at home revolves around Mom. When she is cranky, the kids (or fellow employees) get cranky. Her boss depends on her to stay up, alert, and positive.

14. Knows the etiquette rules of entertaining, planning meetings, dining, and other areas which she will be expected to handle with ease.

15. Uses ingenuity to work around obstacles.

Linda, an executive secretary, is an example of a quality secretary who uses this last point to get answers. Her boss, Mr. Blank, is so busy that it is difficult for even her to see him. His schedule changes radically. He can be told in the middle of a board meeting to fly out somewhere that afternoon.

Rather than becoming frustrated, Linda uses a method she devised for communication convenient to both her and her boss. When she has questions, she inputs them into Mr. Blank's personal office computer, then puts an asterisk on his daily calendar. When he sees the asterisk, he checks his computer for her questions.

Qualities of a Good Employee
In His Relationship with His Boss

1. Respects the boss and abides by his authority as long as he works under him.

2. Shows respect to the boss at all times, never contradicts him (even jokingly) or interrupts him.

3. Takes the cue of how to act from his boss. Knows that if his boss jokes with him, it is fine to follow that lead. But if his boss is seriously working with him on a project, he should remain serious as well.

4. Never tries to act as if he is on the same level as his boss.

The following story is an example of what a young executive should *not* do when with a senior executive.

During the early years of our marriage, my husband Doug and I were invited to a company banquet designed to recognize young up-and-coming executives who had met their sales goals for the year. The president of the company flew in for the event. Doug and I, along with two other couples, were to be seated at his table.

We were sent a memorandum listing the president's hobbies and other items of interest ahead of time so that we could easily carry on a conversation at dinner.

The night of the banquet, Doug and I were seated at the extreme opposite end of the table from the president. As was the natural thing to do, the president turned to the young man on his left and began making conversation. The young man immediately began talking with the president about how flying was his favorite hobby. Flying had been listed as one of the president's hobbies on the memorandum.

After talking with the young man for some time about the subject, the president graciously turned to the young man on his right and asked him some questions. That young man immediately began a long conversation with the president about skiing, another of the topics listed on the memorandum.

After a while, the president tried to throw the ball of conversation over to our court to include us, but no sooner than my husband or I would start to say something, one of the two men would interrupt and take the ball of conversation back. It became almost a game of seeing who could impress the president the most with his knowledge of subjects in common.

At the end of the evening, the president turned to one of the young men and asked, "What do you see as the direction for this company?"

The young man was feeling so comfortable with how much the president had been talking to him, that he crossed his leg in a casual position, then aggressively leaned forward and said, "Well, Mr. _____, when I am president of this company..." and proceeded to list a number of things he intended to do!

Without even knowing all the rules myself at the time, I was totally embarrassed for a young executive to act in such a way. If he had followed just the one rule, "Do unto others as you would have them do unto you," he would have never tried to put himself on the senior executive's level or used such aggressive body language to cause such an uncomfortable situation.

One executive told me of a situation in which an employee was disrespectful in front of a client.

"One day I was coming back into the office with a client from a business luncheon. An employee kiddingly said in front of the client, 'It must be nice to take two-hour lunches.' I was embarrassed for the employee and for my client."

Once again, if the employee had just followed the golden rule, he would have saved his boss and himself a great deal of embarrassment.

Questions and Answers

Q.   I cannot respect my boss and his ethics. He slanders and uses foul language around the office. He does not seem to respect our clients and I often have to cover for him in returning phone calls, etc. I love my job, but find it difficult to be comfortable in my working situation. What should I do?

A.   You always have two options — to stay or to leave. If you choose to stay you owe your respect to your boss even if you feel it is undeserved. Watch for opportunities to talk one-on-one with him, and tell him about some of your discontent when you sense the timing is right.

If you do this, realize it could come out well with both of you having open communication. Or be ready to accept the fact that he may not be willing to see his shortcomings and you might have to change positions. Open communication is important when you are working in a close relationship at the office. All you can do is try to give him your ideas and hope they are accepted.

Q.   I am an easygoing type of employer. I want my employees to feel comfortable with me and I try to treat them as friends. Sometimes, when I am very serious with someone, he takes it lightly and doesn't seem to know when to joke and when to treat me as boss. How can I remain who I am and yet maintain a boss/employee relationship?

A.   It is wonderful of you to be the considerate boss you obviously are with your employees. Yet, somehow you must have discernment as to when to joke with them and be casual and when to remain the boss with expectations of total productivity from them. Perhaps the personal times should be kept outside business hours, such as on breaks, at lunch, or before the day gets going. During the productive hours of the day, remain business-like and the employees will follow your lead.

Q. As a manager who is including a staff person in a meeting with clients, what can you do if the staff person interjects his opinions when they are not wanted and embarrasses your company?

A. The staff person probably is not trying to be assertive, but wants to show he has something to say. I would take him aside later and explain that in certain situations (and give him examples) he should not give opinions unless asked and unless discussed before the meeting.

Showing Appreciation

In any business relationship, finding creative ways of showing appreciation is an especially touching way of showing you care.

I know of an executive who shows his appreciation in a creative way to secretaries who are especially accommodating. Once a month the executive hires a manicurist who goes from office to office on a particular day to give the secretaries a manicure at an appointed time as a way of saying "thank you."

B, C, D.

Part VIII
Travel

Travel

A junior executive who is traveling with a senior executive should:

A.   Assist with the details of travel arrangements such as checking in and out of the hotel and tipping.

B.   Use the time in between meetings to ask the senior executive detailed questions about different phases of business.

C.   Allow the senior executive to choose a seat first when entering a car or limousine.

D.   On a corporate jet, board after the senior executive and wait to be told where to be seated.

Answers appear on p. 199.

24
Air Travel

A woman wrote a letter to the mayor of her city and stated: "In our airport it's hard to find out information — even the location of the baggage claim — or to find a policeman, if you need one. There aren't any niceties to welcome strangers. No wonder our city is considered unfriendly!"

The mayor's office wrote the woman back to say that her comments were appreciated. And today that airport is filled with signs, information people, and recordings welcoming air travelers to the city. We as travelers can take a cue from this story.

Twenty years ago, the method of travel most often used by business people, flying, was a luxury. Now air travel is not as much fun as it once was — flights are packed, people in a hurry tend to be rude. Today travel is often an inconvenience.

Recently I was traveling on an overbooked flight. Most of the passengers were people who had been scheduled on a flight canceled the night before because of a snowstorm.

Even while boarding our flight that morning, the people were still angry. At the end of the flight, a woman almost ran over me as we prepared to deplane. When it was my turn to get in line, she did not give me a chance to get out of my seat and pushed me.

I could have become angry and let that incident upset me for the rest of the day and maybe for weeks afterwards. But I caught myself (not that I always do), and thought, "The poor thing, she's had a bad day." I did not think another thing about the incident. Had I reacted negatively, I could have started a bad verbal exchange with her, and I needed to be positive for my speaking engagement!

Those of us whose business lives include flying often face a decision: we can make traveling a positive or negative experience. To make it a positive experience, we must keep in mind the reasons that we are traveling — the meeting or speaking engagement for which we need to stay positive and sharp — and the good attitude we must project to our colleagues, rather than allowing any incidents that do not really matter to upset us.

If we begin taking little annoyances as personal affronts, we will be out of character when trying to attend to the business ahead of us. As we travel, we need to put on defensively an armor of maintaining a professional image. Otherwise, we might find it easy to digress and act like some of our fellow travelers — impatient and rude.

"Niceties" turned stopping over in the airport mentioned above into a pleasant experience. In the same way, our use of good manners, and a special effort to treat others as we would want to be treated, can turn our business trips into positive experiences both for ourselves and for others. And niceties are especially appreciated in situations where they are usually not found. Because good manners are not used as often as they should be by travelers, the good manners we use will be especially appreciated.

Traveling by Air — Courtesies

Because everyone is in close contact for a long period of time, be especially considerate of others.

• Remember to say "excuse me" in the aisles and "please" and "thank you." Flight attendants are trained to be courteous no matter what happens. They will especially appreciate someone being courteous to them.

If you want a smile from other passengers, give a smile. When treated politely, people usually respond in the same way.

• Do not bring too many carry-on items. You will make both your seatmates and yourself uncomfortable.

• Always leave the lavatory clean and make your visits brief. A woman who wants to adjust her make-up can do so in her seat.

• If in an aisle seat, get up to let your seatmates pass. It is difficult to climb over people.

• If sitting in economy class, do not recline your seat. The seats are too close for the person behind you to be comfortable when your seat is reclined.

• When seated by someone who wants to talk when you need to work or simply do not feel like talking, answer with short, but polite responses. If you are not already working on papers or reading, take some material from your briefcase and begin working on it. You can apologize for not having time to chat. You might offer the person a magazine.

When the meal is served, be gracious by carrying on a conversation, then return to your work after eating.

Smoking

• On domestic flights, pipe or cigar smoking is not allowed, even in the smoking section. On foreign flights, it is often allowed. To handle a problem with a smoker, quietly notify the flight attendant.

Landing Safety

• Immediately after landing, people often stand up and start removing things from the overhead compartments. Because of this, a number of passengers are injured every year. All people should remain in their seats until the plane comes to a complete stop.

25
Traveling With Colleagues or Alone

Traveling With a Senior Executive

As a junior executive, you should aide a senior executive as much as possible. Assist with details such as checking in and out of the hotel and tipping. Do not engage the senior executive in long conversations unless he encourages you.

When getting into a car or limousine, wait to take a seat until the senior executive has chosen one first.

When flying on a corporate jet, always arrive early. Board after the senior executive or host, and sit where you are shown. Do not ask for refreshments unless they are offered. Be neat when eating and drinking and do not litter.

Always thank the crew as you leave. Write a thank you note to the executive who reserved you a seat on the flight.

Male and Female Colleagues
Traveling Together

When men and women travel together on business, certain behavior should be followed for the sake of reputation. Here are some basic guidelines.

1. Avoid flirtations, no matter how innocent. They may be misunderstood.

2. At the first sign of inappropriate behavior on the part of your colleague, take some action to end it right there. Then act as though the incident never happened to preserve the working relationship.

3. When business needs to be conducted, arrange to work in a public place such as the hotel lobby or restaurant.

4. A man and a woman should be separately responsible for expenses.

• A woman executive should travel with advance money or use her own money to pay for her expenses, then later be reimbursed by her company.

• If a male and female colleague dine together, they should each use their own expense account to pay for their meal.

• A woman executive should tip for her own baggage handling and airport limousine fee.

• Either the man or woman may pay shared taxi fares, then reimbursements should be made for filing individual expense reports.

A Woman Traveling Alone
on Business

Business travel is a special concern for women. Your travel objectives, however, are the same as for the male executive. You have a job to do and you want to do that job efficiently, minimizing time, energy, cost, and aggravation while maximizing your comfort and enjoyment.

Safety/Danger Zones and Times

When traveling alone, establish safety / danger zones and times. For instance:

Safety zones — your hotel room, the front desk, the coffee shop.

Danger zones — the bar, elevators, stairways, parking lot, garages, and hallways. While in these areas, stay alert to signs of danger.

Safety times — daylight. Make your flight reservations early in the day and arrive at your destination before dark.

Dining

Many women who travel tell me that they do not feel comfortable dining alone in a restaurant and, for that reason, often use room service. By eating in their room, they accomplish more work, but often would rather be among people.

As a businesswoman, you have every right to dine alone in a restaurant. Walk in confidently and say, "Dinner for one, please." The key is to act as if you belong there and deserve the same good service given to everyone else.

If the service is good, leave a tip of 15 to 20 percent. Also keep in mind when figuring the tip that there is no such thing as a table for one. If your waiter had served two people, the check would have been twice as much and the tip would have been twice as big.

If you intend to be left alone while dining, try the following:

1. Remain businesslike in your dress and behavior. You could even carry your briefcase or other papers. Both actions clearly give the message that you are a professional businesswoman and are involved in reviewing business while you are eating.

2. Handle intrusions diplomatically.

If someone you are not interested in talking to starts talking to you, smile pleasantly and answer him, then take papers from your briefcase and begin working.

If someone asks to join you and you want to refuse, simply say, "No thanks."

If you prefer not to travel alone, look into traveling with someone else in your organization or with a group. You might be able to travel with other females from other companies who are going to the same place at the same time.

Hotels

Precautions

When staying in a hotel or motel, both men and women should take certain precautions, but women should be especially careful.

1. Avoid exposing your room number in a public setting such as in a restaurant when signing your check.

2. Always double lock your room door and put on the chain. Check balcony doors and windows. If one is broken or cannot be locked, call for a maintenance man to fix it or show you how to lock it.

3. Do not enter your room if people are standing idly nearby. Walk past your door, then return later. When leaving your room, look carefully down the hallway as a precaution. Always check to be sure the door has locked behind you.

Tipping

When checking out of a hotel, tip the bellman $1 per bag or $1 for the first bag and $.50 for smaller bags. Rather than tipping per bag, you may give a general tip of $3 to $5.

Tip the valet attendant who brings your car $2 minimum — $1 for bringing the car and $1 per bag.

A, C, D.

YES! I'm interested in your services/products.

Name: _____
Title:
Company/ _____
Organization: _____
Address: _____
City/State: _____Zip: _____

PLEASE CALL ME AT: _____

PLEASE SEND INFORMATION REGARDING:

    __ KEYNOTE SPEECHES
    __ SEMINARS

PLEASE SEND THE FOLLOWING PRODUCTS:

    __ CORPORATE PROTOCOL CASSETTE TAPE SERIES - 4 PAK @ $49.95
        (includes book, value added information on tapes)

    __ BOOK - SEASONS OF SUCCESS: An Image of Excellence @ $5.00

    __ Total Ordered $_____

__ Invoice Me

__ Enclosed is My Check or Money Order

(Allow 2 weeks for delivery)

VALERIE AND COMPANY
13140 Coit Road, Suite 522
Dallas, Texas 75240
(214) 644-0444

References

Baldrige, Letitia. *Letitia Baldrige's Complete Guide to Executive Manners.* Edited by Sandi Gelles-Cole. New York: Rawson Associates, 1985.

Stewart, Marjabelle Young; Faux, Marian G. *Executive Etiquette.* New York: St. Martin's Press, 1979.

Valerie Grant-Sokolosky, a national keynote speaker and author, specializes in topics including:

- Professional and Corporate Image
- Corporate Protocol/Ethics
- Building Sales/Client Relationships

Her two books — *Seasons of Success* and *Corporate Protocol, a Brief Case for Business Etiquette* are distributed worldwide and her cassette programs are included in the Nightingale-Conant seminar company.

Range of accomplishments include an early career at age 16 in radio and television. As a regular columnist for major newspapers and trade magazines, she appears often on talk shows. Her full-service consulting firm designs and presents corporate training programs.

Recognitions:
- One of 2,000 National Women of Achievement
- Outstanding Woman of Texas
- Member of Leadership Dallas
- Outstanding Delta Zeta of the Year

Board Positions:
- Sales & Marketing Executives
- Miss America — Miss Texas Pageant
- The Fashion Group International
- Image Industry Council, International

Affiliations:
- National Speakers Association
- Leadership Dallas
- Junior League

For information regarding speaking or training, please contact:

Valerie and Company
13140 Coit Road, Suite 522
Dallas, Texas 75240

Index